"At the bottom of many of the controversies plaguing the church today is the question of authority. Doctrinal errors and heresies thrive where Scripture is ignored or rejected. But God has spoken, and the Bible is His *Final Word*. No one in our generation has understood this more clearly nor defended it more courageously than John MacArthur. In this book he demonstrates—from Scripture itself—how and why God's written Word must be recognized as the ultimate authority for people who confess Jesus as Lord. Such commitment to Scripture must never be assumed or else it will soon be lost. Read this book, and use it to help others understand how to live faithfully under the authority of Jesus Christ."

—Dr. Tom Ascol
Pastor, Grace Baptist Church, Cape Coral, Fla.
Executive director, Founders Ministries

"*Final Word* is a profound and, unfortunately, very necessary book. I say 'unfortunately' because this book addresses issues that have been raised and responded to for generations. The attacks to which it responds are neither new nor sophisticated. And that is what makes its necessity unfortunate. It is unfortunate that the enemies of the Bible must be confronted yet again. However, confront them we must, and that is precisely what John MacArthur does in *Final Word*. May this profound and necessary book bolster your faith in God's Word as it answers questions, dispels myths, and reasserts the inerrancy, sufficiency, and beauty of the Scriptures."

—Dr. Voddie Baucham
Dean of the seminary
African Christian University, Lusaka, Zambia

"In every generation, God raises up one primary champion to contend for the authority and sufficiency of the written Word of God. In the sixteenth century, that valiant individual was Martin Luther. In the nineteenth century, the leading figure was Benjamin Breckinridge Warfield. I believe history will reveal that for the twenty-first century, John MacArthur has been that strong man who has stood immovable for the divine inspiration, inerrancy, and authority of Scripture. For more than half a century, MacArthur has advanced to the frontlines in the battle for the Bible and has fought the good fight to defend it against the relentless assaults of radical unbelief. Read this book, *Final Word*, and you will be fortified and emboldened in your faith."

—Dr. Steven J. Lawson
Founder and president
OnePassion Ministries, Dallas

# FINAL WORD

# FINAL WORD

WHY WE NEED THE BIBLE

# JOHN MACARTHUR

 LIGONIER MINISTRIES

*Final Word: Why We Need the Bible*
© 2019 by John MacArthur

Published by Ligonier Ministries
421 Ligonier Court, Sanford, FL 32771
Ligonier.org

Printed in Crawfordsville, Indiana
Lakeside Book Company
0001221
First edition, sixth printing

ISBN 978-1-64289-126-3 (Hardcover)
ISBN 978-1-64289-127-0 (ePub)
ISBN 978-1-64289-128-7 (Kindle)

Cover design: Metaleap Creative
Interior design and typeset: Katherine Lloyd, The DESK

Unless otherwise noted, Scripture quotations are taken from the New American Standard Bible® (NASB), Copyright © 1960, 1962, 1963, 1968, 1971, 1972, 1973, 1975, 1977, 1995 by The Lockman Foundation. Used by permission. www.Lockman.org

Scripture quotations marked ESV are taken from the ESV® Bible (The Holy Bible, English Standard Version®), copyright © 2001 by Crossway, a publishing ministry of Good News Publishers. Used by permission. All rights reserved.

The Library of Congress has cataloged the Reformation Trust edition as follows:
Names: MacArthur, John, 1939- author.
Title: Final word : why we need the Bible / John MacArthur.
Description: Orlando, FL : Reformation Trust Publishing, A Division of Ligonier Ministries, [2019] | Includes index.
Identifiers: LCCN 2018037212| ISBN 9781642891263 (hardcover) | ISBN 9781642891287 (mobi) | ISBN 9781642891270 (ePub)
Subjects: LCSH: Bible--Evidences, authority, etc. | Bible--Use.
Classification: LCC BS480 .M185 2019 | DDC 220.1--dc23
LC record available at https://lccn.loc.gov/2018037212

# CONTENTS

## Chapter One

# THE BIBLE
# IS UNDER ATTACK

Elizabeth Charles, the hymn writer who gave us "Praise Ye the Triune God," was also a novelist. She wrote a work of historical fiction set in early sixteenth-century Germany—the dawn of the Protestant Reformation. Leo X has just issued the papal bull *Decet Romanum pontificem* formally excommunicating Martin Luther. Roman Catholic officials go on a quest to silence Luther's teaching and intimidate his followers. Luther's works are publicly burned. Anyone who admits to being in agreement with him is arrested and charged with heresy. One of the novel's characters is a monk named Fritz who decides to confess his agreement with Luther on the doctrine of justification by faith, even though he knows it means he too will be excommunicated and sent to prison. The character, Fritz, explains his willingness to confess:

> It is the truth which is assailed in any age which tests our fidelity. It is to *confess* we are called, not merely to *profess*.

If I profess, with the loudest voice and the clearest exposition, every portion of the truth of God except precisely that little point which the world and the devil are at that moment attacking, I am not confessing Christ, however boldly I may be professing Christianity. Where the battle rages the loyalty of the soldier is proved; and to be steady on all the battle-field besides is mere flight and disgrace to him if he flinches at that one point.[1]

Fritz's statement reflects Luther's own perspective about the importance of standing firm when a particular point of biblical doctrine is under fierce assault—and especially when the consequences of defending a controversial truth are costly. Such an insight on the Christian's duty to be steadfast and immovable has never been more important than it is today.

Without a doubt, the ground Satan most vigorously and continuously attacks these days is the trustworthiness of Scripture—its authority, sufficiency, inerrancy, integrity, and perspicuity. The battle for the truth is the battle for the Bible, and in this fight God's people cannot flinch. Biblical truth is under relentless and endless assault. And like Luther and the heroes of the early Reformation, we must meet the enemy head-on and be willing to stand and fight for the truth, especially when others avoid or even abandon truth when it becomes controversial.

## Satan's Ancient Strategy

Where did the war for the truth begin? In Genesis 3, we see the first instance of Satan's strategic assault on God's Word:

Now the serpent was more crafty than any beast of the field which the LORD God had made. And he said to the woman, "Indeed, has God said, 'You shall not eat from any tree of the garden'?" The woman said to the serpent, "From the fruit of the trees of the garden we may eat; but from the fruit of the tree which is in the middle of the garden, God has said, 'You shall not eat from it or touch it, or you will die.'" The serpent said to the woman, "You surely will not die! For God knows that in the day you eat from it your eyes will be opened, and you will be like God, knowing good and evil." (Gen. 3:1–5)

Satan earns his title as the "father of lies" (John 8:44) here in Genesis 3. He is the source of the first lie, which was the serpent's falsely telling Eve that God was lying to her. And he has relentlessly continued sowing that same doubt and distrust in God's Word ever since. In fact, the only time Satan is ever consistent is in his lying. Everything in him is lies and deceit.

In the garden, he begins with what sounds like an innocuous question that might come from a disinterested observer. He pretends he is concerned only for Eve's well-being. Soon, any imagined neutrality disappears as he boldly claims to know more than God does. He insinuates that God is wrong and he is right. God may have said that they would die, but Satan assures Eve they won't. This perverse deception that we see in Genesis 3 is repeated throughout history: God says one thing; Satan says God is a liar and counters with a different story.

It is instructive for us to examine Satan's time-tested strategy.

In the garden, he began his campaign with a facade of inno-cence, just asking a simple question: "Indeed, has God said?" (Gen. 3:1). You could actually translate his words as, "So, God has said, has He?" Here we have the first question in the Bible, which introduces the first dilemma in human history. There were no questions or dilemmas before this one. Up to this point, Adam and Eve had walked in perfect fellowship with God. Then there was the first question, and it was about the integrity and honesty of God. This query was designed to start Eve down the path of doubting the truthfulness of what God had said, and doubting God's word is the essence of sin. For the first time, that deadly spiritual force was covertly smuggled into the world.

Satan's lie about God also included a distortion of God's original command: "From any tree of the garden you may eat freely; but from the tree of the knowledge of good and evil you shall not eat, for in the day that you eat from it you will surely die" (Gen. 2:16–17). The devil twisted the positive of God's abundant provision into a negative, perverting and inverting the emphasis to *not eating* and pressing the issue of prohibition. He implied that God's word should be questioned, evaluated, and judged by Eve. He picked at the issue of the limitation that God put on Adam and her, hoping to persuade her that there is a flaw in God's character that makes Him unnecessarily restrictive and narrow. Satan suggested that by restraining their free will, God was withholding some delight from them—that there was some good, some pleasure, some joy, some advanced level of satisfaction or fulfillment He was denying them.

Satan painted God as the One who wanted to take away

their choices, crimp their freedom, and limit their rights. The assumption underneath everything Satan said was that God is not loving and caring—and that if He presents Himself that way, it's a deception, and He cannot be trusted at all. In fact, Satan was subtly suggesting to Eve that *he* was more devoted to her well-being than God was, because he was the one looking out for her full freedom and satisfaction in doing whatever she wanted. He was the one who was committed to her real rights and true happiness. In this way, Satan set loose in her mind the idea that this simple prohibition from God proved a serious divine character defect, casting suspicion on both God's goodness and the trustworthiness of His words.

At this point, Eve wasn't quite ready to cave in, so she clarified God's command: "From the fruit of the trees of the garden we may eat" (Gen. 3:2). In other words, God had certainly put a limitation on them, but there were plenty of alternatives. It's not a strong defense of God; she should have been outraged in her response to the serpent's twisting of His word. After all, she knew God—she was intimately acquainted with His goodness, perfection, and holiness. She knew He had given an unmistakable and unambiguous command, and she also should have been suspicious of a talking snake twisting her Creator's words. Ultimately, she should have made a bold and emphatic defense of God in the face of this attempt to question and undermine His command. She could have responded as Christ did in the face of Satan's attempts to likewise sow doubt in His heart. Christ affirmed His perfect trust in God and the authority and sufficiency of His Word (Matt. 4:1–11). But Eve did not.

Instead, she fell into the trap of her deceiver. She continued, "But from the fruit of the tree which is in the middle of the garden, God has said, 'You shall not eat from it or touch it, or you will die'" (Gen. 3:3). Not only was Eve succumbing to doubt, but she also began to misrepresent God's word herself by adding a word to God's command—the word "touch." That's a clear indication that she accepted the devil's argument that God is restrictive, showing her displeasure with God by making the exaggerated claim that she and Adam couldn't even *touch* the tree. The temptation was successful, and she believed the lie that God was evil in exercising illegitimate and unfair restraint on her and her husband.

This was a pivotal moment in the gestation of sin and the fall of the human race. As soon as she did not completely, wholeheartedly, and unreservedly trust in the word of God as absolutely true and the source of her highest joy, greatest good, deepest satisfaction, broadest pleasure, and most consummate fulfillment—at that moment, the sin of mistrust corrupted her heart. Eating the fruit was the consummation of Adam's and Eve's sin and the event that signified the fall of the human race, but this moment of thought was the first appearance of sin in Eden. Sin arrived when Eve stopped trusting the truthfulness of God's word and began believing that He was wickedly restrictive.

Satan then moved in for a full denial. He knew exactly what she was thinking because of what she said. The serpent boldly, blatantly, and flatly declared to the woman, "You surely will not die!" (Gen. 3:4). He led her to believe that God wanted to rob her of her liberty and impinge on her freedom. God did not tell her the truth, Satan said, assuring her that she wouldn't die. Essentially, he said that what God says cannot be trusted and that He did not have her best interest in mind. His path is not the path to truest fulfillment. And she believed, ever so slightly, that God is flawed, deceptive, and needlessly limiting. God was not only holding back her joy, but He also lied when He said there would be judgment for disobedience.

That, in effect, is the prototype of Satan's big lie—no limits, no consequences, and no judgment. Live any way you desire, without accountability or retribution. Furthermore, he claims, a God who puts such limits on you must not really love you. Satan essentially says: "Do what you want. I won't put any restraints on you. I'm all love, not law. God is all law, not love." And he's been peddling that same lie—with great success— since he confronted Eve in the garden.

At this point, an obvious quandary presents itself: Why would God be like this? Satan said in 3:5, "For God knows that in the day you eat from it your eyes will be opened, and you will be like God, knowing good and evil." This was simply an extension of his assault on the character and nature of God. He effectively told Eve: "God is jealous, envious, and controlling. He knows if you eat from that tree, you will be His equals and share His unfettered freedom. He knows that if you eat from the tree, you will be as free as He is—that you will essentially *be* God. And He can't tolerate rivals." Satan knew this issue personally. It was his desire to be equal with God that led to his being thrown out of heaven and becoming Satan (Ezek. 28:14– 16). And in this crafty conversation with Eve, the frustrated father of lies who was expelled by God brought down the whole human race on the premise that God could not be trusted.

We won't take the time to trace the full flow of the satanic assault on the truth that began in the garden of Eden. However, Scripture reveals throughout redemptive history Satan's uninterrupted attempts to sow error and destroy truth. The Bible chronicles an endless litany of diabolical false prophets, false teachers, liars, false apostles, and deceivers from Genesis to Revelation. And even since the canon was closed and the Word of God was once for all delivered to the saints, the battle has not diminished at all. He always attacks the Bible.

## Friendly Fire

Today, the landscape of the battle for the truth extends far and wide, and it rages on countless fronts. Every attack on the Bible is an attack on divine truth and God's holy nature, no matter where the attack originates. And what is most shocking in this endless battle is how often Scripture is hit by friendly fire.

Perhaps no doctrine has been as consistently assaulted from within the church as the inerrancy of Scripture. Reaching back to the Age of Enlightenment, the integrity and reliability of God's Word have been questioned and denied routinely by critics in the church who have fallen under the sway of worldly wisdom. Some see the Bible as imprecise and unscientific—in particular, they believe the account of God's creative work in Genesis does not hold up against the world's theories on evolution, origins, and the age of the earth. Others simply dismiss

Scripture as outdated and out of step with modern social views on sexuality, marriage, and gender roles.

At the core of the typical objections to God's Word is the issue of inerrancy (the Bible's historical, scientific, and factual accuracy). This is a debate I have been engaged in almost continuously throughout five decades of ministry. In 1978, I had the privilege of convening with more than two hundred evangelical pastors and theologians in Chicago at the International Council on Biblical Inerrancy. There, we drafted and signed the Chicago Statement on Biblical Inerrancy in defense of Scripture's comprehensive integrity and infallibility.

But many in the church remained unmoved in their denial of Scripture's inerrancy. They argued—incongruously—that God's Word could be authoritative even if it wasn't entirely true. Borrowed from the secular academy, that corrupt concept of Scripture was particularly influential at seminaries and Bible colleges. I was even invited to debate the issue at Fuller Theological Seminary, where two faculty members—Jack Rogers and Donald McKim—had been promoting their unorthodox ideas. Their subtle but dangerous denial of inerrancy is spelled out in the introduction to their influential book *The Authority and Interpretation of the Bible*:

> The central Christian tradition included the concept of accommodation. This was a grateful acknowledgment that God had condescended and adapted himself in Scripture to our human ways of thinking and speaking. God's ways are not our ways and his thoughts are

not our thoughts. But for our sakes, God became intelligible to us in the incarnation, the person of Christ, as well as in the normal language and experiences of human beings recorded in the Bible. Through both of these very human means, the Good News of God's salvation is clearly shown. To erect a standard of modern, technical precision in language as the hallmark of biblical authority was totally foreign to the foundation shared by the early church.[2]

Of course, we understand that the Lord, in communicating His revelation through Spirit-inspired human authors, graciously accommodates His truth to our fallen, finite minds. That's why the authors of Scripture use figures of speech, symbols, and anthropomorphic expressions to illustrate and illuminate complex biblical truth. However, the kind of accommodation Rogers, McKim, and others refer to goes a fatal step further, introducing error into the biblical text by way of its human authors. From their perspective, Scripture's lack of "technical precision in language" is the answer for any discrepancies between the Genesis account and modern theories about the origins of the universe, and every other biblical claim the world calls into question.

But a flawed and erroneous Bible is no longer the authoritative Word of God. And that low view of Scripture has successively given license to liberal theologians, militant feminists, homosexuals, and many others intent on assaulting the authority and relevance of God's Word. Moreover, the view of Scripture as not inerrant has proven to be a slippery slope—one that frequently leads to the outright denial of the Bible and to apostasy. Assaults on Scripture are deadly, no matter where they come from.

# Modern Battlegrounds in an Ancient War

Such instances of friendly fire are all the more tragic when we consider all the ways Satan is actively attacking the church's confidence in the authority and sufficiency of God's Word today. His all-out assault spans several battlefronts. He doesn't need the assistance of heedless believers too.

In order to withstand Satan's attempts to shake our confidence in God's Word, it's helpful for us to consider and categorize his primary points of attack.

## *Critics*

First, God's Word is under constant assaults from critics. Higher textual criticism poisoned the well, killing churches across Europe and America, by denying the inspiration and reliability of Scripture. And while the true church has thoroughly answered the specious claims of higher criticism and theological liberalism, the doubts they sowed continue to spring up in the church like weeds. We see contemporary proof of their lingering influence every year, as new books and documentaries purport to uncover "the real Jesus" or unlock the secrets codes supposedly embedded in the Bible.

One of the most concerted assaults on the authenticity of God's Word came in the form of the Jesus Seminar. The seminar was ostensibly an effort to identify the historical Jesus by determining the historicity of the words and deeds attributed to Him in the Gospels. Made up of more than two hundred fellows (with varying academic credentials and theological expertise), the Jesus Seminar sat in judgment over the integrity and reliability of Scripture for more than twenty years. And the group's findings reveal just how little respect they had for the authority of God's Word. According to the seminar's website, "In the judgment of the Jesus Seminar Fellows, about 18 percent of the sayings and 16 percent of the deeds attributed to Jesus in the gospels are authentic."[3]

That's more than 80 percent of the Gospels swept aside and eliminated as fiction. Among the ousted quotes are Matthew 5:11, "Blessed are you when people insult you and persecute you, and falsely say all kinds of evil against you because of Me," and Mark 10:32–34, in which Jesus foretold His crucifixion. In fact, the Jesus Seminar jettisoned all of the Lord's prophetic words and His apocalyptic teaching, along with the entire gospel of John—except 4:44, which was deemed "possibly authentic," and ironically reminds us "a prophet has no honor in his own country." Seminar founder Robert Funk argued for the dismissal of John's gospel on the grounds that "Jesus speaks regularly in adages or aphorisms, or in parables, or in witticisms created as a rebuff or retort in the context of dialogue or debate. It is clear he did not speak in long monologues of the type found in the Gospel of John."[4]

How did these twentieth-century critics determine what Jesus said and did? Through a simple majority vote. They kept anything that didn't offend their politically correct sensibilities and theologically liberal ideologies, and they eliminated everything else. That includes all of Christ's calls for repentance and His prophecies of the judgment to come. Gone, too, are all Christ's affirmations of His deity, along with all His miracles that proved those claims. Their copious edits to the Gospels turned the Son of God into a superficial sage. In the end, the Jesus Seminar was nothing more than a deceitful exercise in biblical redaction and godless skepticism—a coordinated assault on the person of Christ and the Word of God, disguised as an academic pursuit.

Other critical assaults on Scripture attack not the authenticity of the text itself but rather the meaning of the language the Bible frequently employs. In a now-infamous article for *Christianity Today*, Robert Brow described what he called the "new-model evangelicalism":

> One of the most obvious features of new-model evangelicalism is an emphasis on recalling the warmth of a family relationship when thinking about God. It prefers to picture God as three persons held together in a relationship of love. The Father, Son, and Holy Spirit, it argues, made humans in their image with a view to bringing many children to glory. So instead of being dragged trembling into a law court, we are to breathe in the atmosphere of a loving family. . . . New-model evangelical theology argues that the Roman law court is the wrong context for understanding the Scriptures.[5]

In essence, Brow was promoting a dynamic shift in how the church interprets and explains key theological concepts. He argued for a reinterpretation of terms such as *faith*, *sin*, and *church*, with their new connotations grounded in fiction and parables rather than the historical context of the biblical authors. Regarding the concept of hell, Brow writes, "In *The Great Divorce*, C.S. Lewis rejected the idea that God sends people to hell by a judicial sentence for failing to hear or understand. His picture of a gray city and the freedom to move into the light of heaven suggested that no one could possibly be in hell who would rather be in heaven. I would identify this understanding as new-model, and suggest that it is now a common assumption of many Christians in thoroughly biblical churches."[6]

Brow's reinterpretation similarly corrupts the biblical notion of God's wrath:

In new-model theology, a fourth term, *wrath*—specifically God's wrath—similarly means something different from the old-model understanding. Wrath connotes not angry punishment, but the bad consequences God assigns, as any loving parent might, to destructive or wrongful behavior. The word *wrath* as used in the Old Testament, it is argued, is not primarily a law-court term. It never means sending people to an eternal hell. In fact, it can simply be translated "bad consequences"—the bad consequences of pestilence, drought, and famine, or the ravages of wild animals and invading armies, experienced in the here and now. Likewise, Jesus spoke of terrible consequences that would come about in the fall of Jerusalem—for his generation.[7]

Brow's point was to eliminate the courtroom imagery from Scripture, to do away with any understanding of guilty sinners' facing the due penalty of their sins and standing before a righteous Judge who demands satisfaction and who offers forgiveness and justification to those who surrender themselves in faith and repentance to Him. In the end, Brow's new model for evangelicalism was rooted not in Scripture but in his own imagination. This was not God as He has revealed Himself in the pages of Scripture but God as Brow would prefer to think of Him, refashioned to fit the priorities and perspectives of a therapeutic culture.

That critical, revisionist perspective didn't begin with Brow, and it didn't end with him, either. Like flotsam from the shipwreck of theological liberalism, countless revisionist movements—like open theism, the emerging church, and the New Perspective on Paul—continue to crash onto the shores of the evangelical church, attacking the authority and integrity of God's Word.

### *Cultists*

Just as devastating are the devilish attacks on Scripture from cultists. A cult, for our purposes, is a religious movement that claims to be a Christian group but that deviates significantly from or outright denies the teachings of Scripture and the historic creeds on crucial points. Groups included in this definition are the Mormons, Jehovah's Witnesses, and Christian Scientists. These groups develop their doctrine through a combination of Scripture-twisting and extrabiblical revelation. Under the leadership of self-proclaimed prophets such as Joseph Smith, Charles Taze Russell, and Mary Baker Eddy, these cults consistently pervert biblical truth, denying the deity of Christ and the gospel of grace. Cult leaders relentlessly attack the truth of Scripture through their singular, authoritative interpretation. It's a tragedy that Satan has had such success in twisting elements of biblical language and leveraging pseudo-Christian imagery to lead men and women away from the truth and into these corrupt cults—usually with deadly results.

On multiple occasions, I have sat across from leading Mormon theologians who wanted to discuss the Bible and our theological differences. Each time, I explained that the only reason I agreed to meet was my hope that God would use me to convince them of the horrible error of their ways and lead them to the knowledge of the truth. And that's really the only valid reason to spend time with cultists. Many in the evangelical world today want believers to sit down and share ideas with Muslims, Roman Catholics, and members of other religions. But the truth of Scripture gains nothing in a dialogue with error. There is no Islamic teaching that will make you a better student of Scripture or Mormon doctrine that will give you new insight into God's Word. Error is not a hermeneutic (see Ps. 1:1–3).

### *Charismatics*

Third, we see constant attacks from Satan against God's Word through the charismatic movement. That is not to say that all charismatics are doing the work of the devil or to condemn the entire movement. Far from it—I believe many of the people who are caught up in charismatic churches are simply deceived believers. They are untrained and unable to distinguish between biblical truth and the lies that dominate the movement.

However, the leaders of the movement—the media faces of the charismatic church worldwide—are a different story. They routinely misinterpret and misapply Scripture. They carelessly deliver false prophecies in God's name. And they hold up their own private visions, dreams, and mental impressions as trustworthy revelation from God, equal and sometimes superior to the Bible. Anytime there is a claim to continuing revelation, the sufficiency and authority of God's Word have been assaulted.

Scripture tells us that God takes such attacks on His Word very seriously. Through the pen of the prophet Jeremiah, the Lord declared His own verdict on those who would pretend to speak for Him:

> Thus says the LORD of hosts,
> "Do not listen to the words of the prophets who are
>     prophesying to you.
> They are leading you into futility;
> They speak a vision of their own imagination,
> Not from the mouth of the LORD.
> They keep saying to those who despise Me,
> 'The LORD has said, "You will have peace"';
> And as for everyone who walks in the stubbornness of
>     his own heart,
> They say, 'Calamity will not come upon you.'

But who has stood in the council of the LORD,
That he should see and hear His word?
Who has given heed to His word and listened?"
(Jer. 23:16–18)

One of the pervasive problems in the church today is the utter gullibility of people who will believe anything and everything a so-called pastor or prophet says. There is a severe lack of noble Bereans, who faithfully tested everything they heard against the standard of Scripture (Acts 17:10–11). Today, countless men and women claim to hear fresh words from God—words that often contradict what His Word actually says, and despite the obvious fact that God wouldn't be talking to those with bad theology and questionable behavior. In spite of their inconsistencies, people foolishly turn out in droves to hear what they have to say. Through the prophet Jeremiah, God disavowed those false prophets. The church today would do well to echo His condemnation:

"I did not send these prophets,
But they ran.
I did not speak to them,
But they prophesied.
But if they had stood in My council,
Then they would have announced My words to My
  people,
And would have turned them back from their evil way
And from the evil of their deeds.
Am I a God who is near," declares the LORD,

"And not a God far off?
Can a man hide himself in hiding places
So I do not see him?" declares the LORD.
"Do I not fill the heavens and the earth?" declares the
    LORD.

"I have heard what the prophets have said who prophesy falsely in My name, saying, 'I had a dream, I had a dream!' How long? Is there anything in the hearts of the prophets who prophesy falsehood, even these prophets of the deception of their own heart, who intend to make My people forget My name by their dreams which they relate to one another, just as their fathers forgot My name because of Baal? The prophet who has a dream may relate his dream, but let him who has My word speak My word in truth. What does straw have in common with grain?" declares the LORD. (Jer. 23:21–28)

God's people ought to be able to discern the difference between His true revelation and the false words of these fraudulent prophets, who invite the judgment of the Lord through their brazen deception.

"Is not My word like fire?" declares the LORD, "and like a hammer which shatters a rock? Therefore behold, I am against the prophets," declares the LORD, "who steal My words from each other. Behold, I am against the prophets," declares the LORD, "who use their tongues and declare, 'The Lord declares.' Behold, I am against those who have prophesied false dreams," declares the LORD, "and related them and led My people astray by their falsehoods and reckless boasting; yet I did not send them or command them, nor do they furnish this people the slightest benefit," declares the LORD. (vv. 29–32)

The Lord concludes His condemnation of the false prophets with a look at the spiritual confusion they sow among their followers. These ancient words are an apt description of problems that pervade the church today—specifically, the proliferation of private revelation, which has left many people without any idea of how to identify the true Word of God.

Now when this people or the prophet or a priest asks you saying, "What is the oracle of the LORD?" then you shall say to them, "What oracle?" The LORD declares, "I will abandon you." Then as for the prophet or the priest or the people who say, "The oracle of the LORD," I will bring punishment upon that man and his household. Thus will each of you say to his neighbor and to his brother, "What has the LORD answered?" or, "What has the LORD spoken?" For you will no longer remember the oracle of the LORD, because every man's own word will become the oracle, and you have perverted the words of the living God, the LORD of hosts, our God. (vv. 33–36)

Countless people under the influence of the charismatic movement are believing false claims of revelation and desperately looking for messages from God that they will never receive. And instead of the fresh revelation they've been promised, they receive messages of deception and false promises from the Enemy—all while they hold a closed Bible in their hands.

## Culture

The culture is another key battleground wherein God's Word is always under attack. Throughout much of the twentieth century, the cultural assault on the truth came in the form of modernism. The modernist, naturalistic worldview claimed that only science can explain reality—that claims of supernatural power and miracles can and should be dismissed out of hand. Obviously, modernism stands in stark opposition to the supernatural truth of Scripture. Yet in the face of modernism's assault on the truth, many churches, seminaries, and even whole denominations rolled over and gave in to this utterly unbiblical worldview.

Modernism was eventually replaced with postmodernism, and today that worldview is similarly corrupting the church and leading to compromise with the godless culture. Unlike modernism, postmodernism does not adhere to one fixed rule to determine universal truth. Instead, it rejects the notion of universal truth altogether. In the postmodern worldview, truth can't be fully known—and it might not exist in the first place. Instead, all truth claims are evaluated subjectively. What's true for one person might not be true for anyone else.

In this plurality of personalized truth, the greatest cultural virtue is tolerance. In the backwards economy of postmodernism, what matters most is one's willingness to tolerate (that is, validate, accommodate, and celebrate) other people's truth claims. This philosophical free-for-all has led to the cultural cesspool we endure today, wherein something as fundamental as one's gender is up for subjective interpretation and redefinition.

Of course, the tenets of postmodernism are diametrically opposed to the Bible, which is absolutely true and, therefore, fundamentally *intolerant*. But that hasn't stopped many in the church from foolishly attempting to blend the two opposing worldviews. The result is what some have called the hermeneutic of humility—the notion that believers shouldn't hold too tightly or dogmatically to an interpretation of God's Word, especially not to the exclusion of other views and perspectives. Such a mind-set undermines the authority and the absolute truth of Scripture, as well as any hope of confronting the spiritual and theological errors of the lost.

The message of the church cannot be dictated by the whims and values of the culture. Sinners can't be coddled into the kingdom. Rebellious unbelief demands confrontation at the point of unbelief. We must not skirt the offense of God's Word if we mean to lead people to faith and repentance—it is exactly at the point where the gospel offends that sinners need to be confronted. True saving faith is impossible if sinners don't yield to the guilt of their sin and submit to the authority of God's Word concerning their condemnation and salvation. We need to be humble, tender, and loving in our evangelism. But we must not be confused into thinking that the goal is anything other than to smash deceptions and torch misunderstandings that nurture unbelief. The postmodern mind-set won't allow that—tolerance cannot abide the absolute truth of God's Word.

## Capricious Approaches

A flippant approach to Scripture is just as dangerous as unabashed unbelief. Satan has launched many attacks on the Bible from the capricious—people who don't study or understand the Word and who lack the proper hermeneutics to do so.

One of the most influential examples of these attacks from several years back is Michael Drosnin's book *The Bible Code*. Drosnin claimed that the text of Scripture contains coded messages that predicted future events, including the assassinations of world leaders and the timing of the Apocalypse. Many other supposedly Christian authors and publishers leapt aboard the bandwagon, creating a deluge of books about all the secret codes and prophecies embedded in the pages of Scripture. Of course, these books are all nonsense—other authors have shown that employing the same interpretive gymnastics will elicit similar "prophecies" from *Moby Dick*. But the vast popularity of these books has signaled a comprehensive assault on the perspicuity of God's Word. And there is no end to the irresponsible misinterpretations of Scripture that are used to bolster lies and produce bad doctrine.

## Carnal Wisdom

Finally, the Word of God is under constant attack from the carnal wisdom of the world. This is the broad category of Satan's attempts to make the truth of Scripture seem unreasonable to sinful people. It's every claim that the book of Genesis can't be trusted because it can't be scientifically proven. It's every objection that God's sovereignty in election is unjust or that it turns mankind into nothing more than preprogrammed automatons. It's the rejection of eternal punishment that results in universalism or annihilationism. And it's the foolish heart of unbelief that argues against the exclusivity of the gospel in favor of a "wider mercy" that paves other avenues for entrance into the kingdom of God.

In essence, carnal wisdom is whatever Satan attempts to stack against the authority and sufficiency of Scripture: so-called science, human reason, and feeble notions of justice and fairness. Satan uses man's inherent pride to undercut the truth and authority of God's Word at every turn.

Those are some of the key categories of Satan's constant assault on the truth. And our responsibility to defend the truth is clearly spelled out in the pages of Scripture. Jude 3 charges us to "contend earnestly for the faith." In 2 Corinthians 10:3–5, Paul charges us to rescue those imprisoned in corrupt ideological fortresses. Put simply, our battle is to bring the truth to people trapped in deadly lies. We must uphold the standard of God's truth, proclaiming its inerrancy, authority, sufficiency, perspicuity, and integrity. The truth is under attack, and that very truth is our only weapon in the ancient war. We must defend the Scripture with the Scripture, rightly interpreted.

## Chapter Two

# THE BIBLE IS TRUTH

Antipathy toward God's Word inherently resides in the hearts of all sinners. This antipathy may even be present in those *within the church*. If there is any doubt about this, it is worth asking why popular evangelicalism's greatest fear is being out of sync with the culture. Pastors and leaders are chasing the culture, so that its trends show up in their churches. They treat this pursuit as a necessary evangelistic strategy. But the only way to be in sync with the culture is to diminish the presence of the Word of God, because unregenerate culture will always be fundamentally and irreconcilably incompatible with the truth of God. By catering to the unchurched or to the unconverted in the church, evangelicalism has been hijacked by legions of carnal spin doctors seeking to convince the world that Christians can be just as inclusive, pluralistic, and open-minded as any postmodern, politically correct worldling.

However, true biblical Christianity requires a denial of every worldly value and behavior, and Christians must be willing to make a commitment to the Word of God, with a full understanding of the implications of doing so. Jesus plainly tells the disciples in John 15:19 that the world will hate them because they are not of this world. God has chosen believers out of the world, and the world hates them. In Luke 6:26, Jesus says, "Woe to you when all men speak well of you, for their fathers used to treat the false prophets in the same way."

Why is the world so fixed in its animosity toward the truth of God? Jesus says in John 7:7, "The world . . . hates Me because I testify of it, that its deeds are evil." Contempt for Scripture is not intellectual; it's moral. As the Lord explained to Nicodemus, "Men loved the darkness rather than the Light, for their deeds were evil" (John 3:19). How tragic for the church to seek to accommodate that worldly affection, since it is impossible by any human method to overcome the sinner's resistance to the truth and the gospel (2 Cor. 3:14). The only time the church has made any spiritual impact on the world is when the people of God have stood firm and have refused to compromise, boldly proclaiming the truth in the face of the world's hostility. In the end, seeking cultural relevance will only result in obsolescence, since tomorrow's generation will inevitably renounce today's fads and philosophies.

In the face of ever-changing cultural trends, the church needs to boldly proclaim the eternal relevance and evergreen applicability of the Word of God. In particular, Christians must embrace and exalt six truths about the Scripture: its objectivity, rationality, veracity, authority, incompatibility, and integrity. These six characteristics help us understand the essential nature of God's Word and help us better minister to a sinful world in desperate need of Scripture's life-transforming truth.

## Objective Truth

First, the Word of God is characterized by objectivity. We must begin by acknowledging that the source of truth is completely outside of us. People may believe or disbelieve the Bible, but no one has the power or the prerogative to establish truth or to change it. It is fixed, once for all—the Word of God is settled forever in heaven. This is profoundly essential.

God wrote a Book—just one Book—and He was able to say everything He wanted to say. He said it without error, without flaw, and without anything omitted or unnecessarily included. It is the truth, the whole truth, and nothing but the truth. And God gave His Book to man through the means of inspiration, by which the Spirit of God moved in human writers who wrote down the very words that God wanted them to write.

That's an important distinction we must not miss—the truth did not come from man. Man may discover, learn, understand, and apply it, but man has nothing to do with its origination. The Apostle Peter—himself one of the inspired biblical authors—wrote that Scripture was not developed by the will of man, but by those "moved by the Holy Spirit" (2 Peter 1:21) to record God's words. No human being has ever had in himself any idea, thought, or experience that determined any divine truth—it all comes from God. No human or angel has ever been, or will ever be, a source for establishing divine truth. It is God's Word alone.

Scripture itself attests to its divine Author. The Old Testament contains more than 3,800 instances in which the writers claim to be speaking the Word of God. In the New Testament, there are more than three hundred such assertions. Paul claims that he received the gospel not from man but from God (Gal. 1:11–12). In 1 Timothy 5:18, Paul quotes Luke's gospel and refers to it as Scripture. In 2 Peter 3:15–16, Peter calls Paul's writings Scripture. And Jude quotes Peter's epistle, signifying similar biblical credibility. Altogether, the Old and New Testaments abundantly testify that they are the true Word of God.

And as the Word of God, the Bible has no expiration date. Peter extolls the timeless quality of Scripture in his first epistle, declaring, "The word of the Lord endures forever" (1 Peter 1:25). Time has no influence on God's Word. Changing philosophies, worldviews, and cultural norms have no effect on it, either. It is utterly unchanging and can never pass away. "Heaven and earth will pass away," Jesus said, "but My words will not pass away" (Luke 21:33).

Perhaps the best way to understand the objective truth of Scripture is to hear the testimony of the One who is most trustworthy—the Lord Jesus Himself. He testified to the truth of God's Word, down to every detail. He said, "It is easier for heaven and earth to pass away than for one stroke of a letter of the Law to fail" (Luke 16:17). He consistently taught that He had come to fulfill the Word of God. In Matthew 5:17, He said, "Do not think that I came to abolish the Law or the Prophets; I did not come to abolish but to fulfill." He affirmed, "All things which are written through the prophets about the Son of Man will be accomplished" (Luke 18:31). Looking ahead to the cross, Jesus said, "The Son of Man is to go, just as it is written of Him" (Matt. 26:24). Later in the chapter, He rebuked Peter for drawing his sword, reminding the impetuous disciple that He could call down legions of angels for assistance if He wished. Explaining that His arrest was part of God's plan, He said, "How then will the Scriptures be fulfilled?" (Matt. 26:54). He even called attention to incredibly specific prophetic details in Scripture. Psalm 22:1 predicted that the Messiah would cry out and say, "My God, My God, why have You forsaken me?" Hanging on the cross, Jesus exclaimed those words verbatim (Matt. 27:46). His life fulfilled everything that was written about Him, thus affirming Scripture's truthfulness.

Scripture testifies to its own inspiration; it is the Word of God, originating outside of man. This is particularly important to understand in a culture dominated by the subjectivity of postmodernism. Truth cannot be subjective; there is no such thing as *your* truth or *my* truth. Truth is forever fixed. Authentic Christianity has always held that Scripture is absolute, objective truth. The Bible is God's truth regardless of whether a person believes, understands, or likes it. It is permanent and universal truth, and therefore, is the same for everyone. Deuteronomy 4:2 and Revelation 22:18–19 warn against adding to or taking away from Scripture, lest one suffer the plagues recorded therein. Proverbs 30:5–6 states: "Every word of God is tested; He is a shield to those who take refuge in Him. Do not add to His words or He will reprove you, and you will be proved a liar." It is God's Word to man; inspired, objective, and absolute truth.

# Rational Truth

We must embrace Scripture not only in terms of objectivity but also in terms of rationality. The objective revelation of God in Scripture is meant to be understood by normal reasoning. It is logical, noncontradictory, and clear. There are no errors, lies, or unsound principles. There are, in reality, no logical contradictions, though to us there may appear to be inconsistencies or paradoxes due to our human limitations. But ultimately, there are no contradictions in Scripture, no fantasies, no absurdities, no inconsistencies, and no myths.

The Word of God contains the actual history of real people told in normal language. And Scripture is to be understood in the same way we would seek to understand anything—by the process of reason. We use reason to solve a math problem, read an engineering schematic, or diagnose an illness. In the same way, Scripture is understood according to the normal patterns of human reason. It is understood by the mind, not by mystical intuition or epiphany.

That doesn't mean that there is no spiritual component to understanding the Bible. As Paul says in 1 Corinthians 2:14, "But a natural man does not accept the things of the Spirit of God, for they are foolishness to him; and he cannot understand them, because they are spiritually appraised." The natural man is unregenerate, and his mind is still darkened by the slavery of sin. It's the illuminating work of the Holy Spirit that brings saving faith and repentance. So while a true understanding of Scripture in all its fullness is limited to believers, the believer still comes to that true understanding through the normal paths of reasoning. In the same way, the unregenerate person is responsible for not believing in God, because he has been given evidence of God's existence that accords with his normal reasoning powers (Rom. 1:18–20). Man is subject to God's wrath because he does not follow the normal path of reason and conscience to recognize God as his Creator, Lawgiver, and Judge. In spite of what the world claims, it is far more reasonable and rational to believe in creation than evolution. Man is culpable before God because he doesn't follow the path of God-given reason to the most obvious reality in the universe—God.

The rationality of Scripture also has implications for believers. We are meant to understand God's Word through reason. In Nehemiah 8, Ezra stood up and read the Scriptures in front of the people for half the day, explaining to them its meaning. In chapter 7, we learn that Ezra read the Scriptures, studied them, lived them, and then preached them. He came to understand Scripture's meaning before explaining it to the people. This is an important point, because so many Christians believe that the true meaning of Scripture falls on an individual through some intuition or experience. They're looking to unlock the rational truth of God's Word through irrational means.

This is another area in which the church cannot afford to mimic or follow the lead of this perishing world. J.P. Moreland describes in vivid terms the dangers a culture faces when it has surrendered reason and critical thinking: "We are staring down the barrel of a loaded gun, and we can no longer afford to act like it's loaded with blanks."[1] He continues:

Our society has replaced heroes with celebrities, the quest for a well-informed character with the search for a flat stomach, substance and depth with image and personality. In the political process, the makeup man is more important than the speech writer, and we approach the voting booth, not on the basis of a well-developed philosophy of what the state should be, but with a heart full of images, emotions, and slogans all packed into thirty-second sound bites. The mind-numbing, irrational tripe that fills TV talk shows is digested by millions of bored, lonely Americans hungry for that sort of stuff.[2]

What Moreland is describing is the massive tidal wave of anti-intellectualism that has overwhelmed much of society today. Tragically, it has flooded into the church, too. Today, many professing believers have no interest in the carefully reasoned study of God's Word, preferring to seek illumination and instruction through alternate means. Some adopt the rituals of pagan religions, while others simply wait to hear the audible voice of the Lord or receive intuitive mental impressions from the Spirit to interpret the Bible.

That mystical approach to God and His truth is inherently irrational. In fact, the pursuit of private, subjective interpretation effectively denies both the objectivity and rationality of God's truth. It also denies the sufficiency of His inspired Word, presuming that there is more we need to know than what God has placed in Scripture. In the end, this anti-intellectual search for truth often leads to the kind of chaos we see dominating the charismatic movement. For others, it leads to disappointment, despair, and apostasy.

God had a purpose when He gave us the capacity for rational thought. If we want to know Him and understand what He has revealed in His Word, we must approach Scripture rationally, following the normal processes of logic and reason with sound hermeneutics to come to a true understanding of its meaning. The rationality of Scripture is actually a great blessing. It means that instead of a multitude of elusive, scattered, subjective interpretations, there is a fixed, consistent meaning to God's Word for everyone to know with settled confidence.

## Trustworthy Truth

Third, the Word of God is characterized by veracity—it is completely accurate and trustworthy. In 2 Timothy 3:16, Paul writes, "All Scripture is breathed out by God" (ESV). Because the Bible is the very breath of "the God of truth" (Isa. 65:16), we can have confidence that it is utterly trustworthy. Psalm 12:6 proclaims, "The words of the LORD are pure words; as silver tried in a furnace on the earth, refined seven times." This same idea is repeated throughout Psalm 119: God's Word is truth, His commandments are truth, the sum of His Word is truth, all of His ordinances endure forever, and all of His precepts are sure.

Scripture is entirely true, and it contains all the truth necessary for the life of faith. God did not hold back or hide any necessary revelation. Paul makes that very point in his epistle to Timothy: "All Scripture is inspired by God and profitable for teaching, for reproof, for correction, for training in righteousness; so that the man of God may be adequate, equipped for every good work" (2 Tim. 3:16–17). God's Word is uniquely suited to accomplish His intentions for salvation, sanctification, and glorification; it supplies everything we need for life and godliness in this world and hope for the life to come.

Moreover, it is the truth by which all other spiritual and theological truth claims are measured. That's why the hard work of faithful interpretation is so vital, and why God gave pastors and teachers to the church. The truth can be known only if the correct meaning of the text is known.

Today, the church is overrun with false shepherds peddling faulty interpretations of Scripture that are not God's Word. They will tell you that Scripture is all about improving your relationships, soothing your emotional wounds, enriching you financially, and meeting a host of other felt needs. But those are devilish lies meant to cripple your confidence in God's Word when it inevitably fails to do what it was never intended to do.

The purpose of God's Word is to deposit life-transforming truth into the mind. We cannot know the truth of a passage until we understand the accurate interpretation of the passage. We need to be careful and thorough students of all Scripture, confident in its divine authorship and dependent on the Holy Spirit's illuminating work in bringing us to a clear understanding of God's revealed truth.

## Authoritative Truth

Believers must also embrace and submit to the authority of Scripture. God's Word is the final authority in His church—no pastor or pope sits in judgment of it. Peter refers to Scripture as the "utterances of God" (1 Peter 4:11), meaning it is the very words from the mouth of God. Paul says that believers "have the mind of Christ" (1 Cor. 2:16). That isn't some kind of gnostic higher knowledge, attained through mystical or subjective means. It means the mind of Christ is displayed for us in the pages of God's Word. If anyone wants to know what the Lord thinks about anything, he simply needs to open the Bible. All the insight we need has been delivered to us in the authoritative Word of God.

However, we live in a day when people do not respond well to authority. The baffling reality is that churches today are filled with people who want to look anywhere but Scripture to find God. They want to identify Him allegorically in movies, on TV, and throughout pop culture, as if those instances can prick the conscience of the unsaved world in ways Scripture cannot. They think it sounds spiritual to ask, "What would Jesus do?" But they never open their Bibles to study who He is or what He did.

Others reject the hard truths of the gospel that offend worldly sensibilities, preferring to twist Scripture into the therapeutic language of our culture. Some simply ignore portions of the Bible altogether, writing them off as outdated and irrelevant to modern readers. God's people must not be so careless or capricious with

His Word. As Charles Spurgeon rightly explained, there is no other reliable source of truth to which we can cling:

> "Thus saith the Lord" is the only authority in God's Church. When the tabernacle was pitched in the wilderness, what was the authority for its length and breadth? Why was the altar of incense to be placed here, and the brazen laver there? Why so many lambs or bullocks to be offered on a certain day? Why must the passover be roasted whole and not sodden? Simply and only because God had shown all these things to Moses in the holy mount; and thus had Jehovah spoken, "Look that thou make them after their pattern, which was showed thee in the mount." It is even so in the Church at the present day; true servants of God demand to see for all Church ordinances and doctrines the express authority of the Church's only Teacher and Lord. They remember that the Lord Jesus bade the apostles to teach believers to observe all things whatsoever he had commanded them, but he neither gave to them nor to any men power to alter his own commands. The Holy Ghost revealed much of precious truth and holy precept by the apostles, and to his teaching we would give earnest heed; but when men cite the authority of fathers, and councils, and bishops, we give place for subjection, no, not for an hour. They may quote Irenaeus or Cyprian, Augustine or Chrysostom; they may remind us of the dogmas of Luther or Calvin; they may find authority in

Simeon, or Wesley, or Gill—we will listen to the opinions of these great men with the respect which they deserve as men, but having so done, we deny that we have anything to do with these men as authorities in the Church of God, for there nothing has any authority, but "Thus saith the Lord of hosts." Yea, if you shall bring us the concurrent consent of all tradition—if you shall quote precedents venerable with fifteen, sixteen, or seventeen centuries of antiquity, we burn the whole as so much worthless lumber, unless you put your finger upon the passage of Holy Writ which warrants the matter to be of God. You may further plead, in addition to all this venerable authority, the beauty of the ceremony and its usefulness to those who partake therein, but this is all foreign to the point, for to the true Church of God the only question is this, is there a "Thus saith the Lord" for it? And if divine authority be not forthcoming, faithful men thrust forth the intruder as the cunning craftiness of men.[3]

God's people need to submit faithfully to the authority of all Scripture and to the sanctifying work the Spirit accomplishes through it in our lives.

## Incompatible Truth

One primary element of submitting to Scripture's authority is recognizing its incompatibility with false teaching and religious error. If the Word of God is the only truth that speaks authoritatively, then it is incompatible with contradicting ideas. First John 2:21 plainly states, "No lie is of the truth." Paul's stern warning to the Galatians illustrates the danger of blending God's truth with error: "But even if we, or an angel from heaven, should preach to you a gospel contrary to what we have preached to you, he is to be accursed!" (Gal. 1:8). As mentioned in chapter 1, the truth of the gospel doesn't gain anything through dialogue with false religion. Tolerance toward people is a good and biblical virtue, but tolerance toward false teaching is sin. Paul rhetorically illustrated the foolishness of forging alliances between truth and error in his second epistle to the Corinthians: "What fellowship has light with darkness? Or what harmony has Christ with Belial, or what has a believer in common with an unbeliever?" (2 Cor. 6:14–15).

For decades, many in the church have attempted to build alliances across religious lines to combat various social issues. But such accords lead to confusion about what the mission field is that we've been called to reach with the gospel. Moreover, social change is not God's ultimate goal for His church. The Lord did not redeem us from the due penalty of our sins just for the sake of opposing homosexual marriage, overturning abortion laws, or some other attempt to redeem the culture from injustice and evil. Of course, we need to vigorously oppose evil, but we need to do it in a way that does not compromise the truth or give credibility to false religion or false teachers in the process. Submitting to the authority of God's Word means recognizing that it is utterly incompatible with error and living accordingly as a separate people.

## Consistent Truth

Finally, believers need to embrace and exalt the integrity of Scripture. God did not intend for His Word to be subdivided, excerpted, and wrenched out of context. The Bible speaks with consistent authority and perpetual relevance in all matters. It does not require correction, innovation, or editorial oversight.

The key to the Reformation was biblical preaching, and that is always the case with revival. The church flourishes when biblical doctrine is faithfully preached from Bible texts. At such times, the truth of God's Word is properly adorned, as the Spirit originally intended it.

But there are times that are dominated by excusing the Bible's supposed irrelevance. People say, "We believe the doctrines of the Bible, but most people just do not identify with its old language and old stories from an agrarian time period." So they argue that the truths of Scripture must be placed in a contemporary package to better reach people. This, in essence, is to say that we have a more effective way to reach people than the Holy Spirit had in authoring the Scripture.

One current advocate of such proud hubris is Andy Stanley, the pastor of one of the largest churches in America; he has encouraged believers to "unhitch the Christian faith" from the Old Testament.[4] He had previously admonished pastors and teachers to never say, "The Bible says."[5] The result is that biblical doctrine is stripped of its biblical attire and dressed in faddish contemporary fashion. Such meddling is an assault on the power and authority of the Bible. God knew how He wanted His doctrine dressed, and people do not have the liberty to rearrange the wardrobe.

Once such ideas become entrenched, doctrine degrades until it flatly contradicts the Bible. This accurately describes the state of many churches today, where the man-centered, therapeutic doctrine they preach flies in the face of the biblical text.

The call for us today is to return to the doctrine of the Bible as God has intended it to be presented. God has set forth His truth in His chosen biblical contexts, proportions, and relations, and in such stories, parables, analogies, and narratives. He knows what suits the soul of man, and under the work of the Spirit of God, no other forms can supersede or improve on the Word of God. It is characterized by objectivity, rationality, veracity, authority, incompatibility, and integrity.

If God's people want to fulfill their calling to be salt and light in this sinful world, they must cultivate a high view of His Word. The church must embrace and proclaim Scripture in its fullness, boldly holding it forth as God's standard for life and godliness.

## Chapter Three

# THE BIBLE IS AUTHORITATIVE

We live in a skeptical age when it comes to Scripture. While there have always been those who questioned the authority and authenticity of God's Word, the church itself was not home to doubters and skeptics. The staunch anti-authority trend we see among professing believers today began in the eighteenth century and the post-Reformation Enlightenment—during the ascendancy of human reason—when skeptics and critics brought the legitimacy of God's Word under widespread attack. Today, we're dealing with the devastating destruction that has accumulated in just a few centuries due to viewing the Bible as something less than the inerrant, authoritative Word of God.

## Inerrancy in the Pew

The authority and inerrancy of Scripture are fundamental doctrines, yet we have an entire generation of professing

Christians who are neither committed to those dogmas nor able to fight to defend them. Most could not articulate a case for biblical authority or defend why every word of God is true—whether internally from the text of Scripture, or externally from the validations of fulfilled prophecy and reason. Many cannot give a clear defense of why it is necessary to have an inerrant Scripture in order for the Holy Spirit to do His work of saving and sanctifying. Though these are foundational realities, too many Christians seem indifferent to these essentials.

Congregations sit listening to sermons from pastors who have been conditioned to elevate methodology, cultural cues, and entertainment in order to attract a crowd rather than to serve an assembly of true worshipers who are able to understand, articulate, and defend the truth of God revealed in Scripture. While a focus on methodology does not necessarily deny the authority of Scripture, there is a de facto denial of Scripture's supremacy when it is set aside for other means and methods. The Bible is regularly treated superficially and routinely taken out of context, resulting in a generation that has no expectation that the preacher would handle the Word of God accurately. Rather, people are trained to treat the Bible like a book that they are free to manipulate for their own ends, which ultimately both exposes and perpetuates their low view of Scripture.

The Bible is frequently brutalized as people ride over the top of it and pluck off what they want. We must understand that the Bible is divinely reasonable, rational, sensible, and linear. Its arguments were divinely authored and supernaturally delivered to us. Simply bouncing across the top and telling stories about it misses the profound reasoning of the mind of God. The Bible reveals God to us in a way that can be grasped and by which we can be transformed, verse by verse and word by word. When believers are caught up into the highest reaches of God's carefully crafted, inspired revelation, the results are life transforming.

The only One who has the right to speak to His people with authority is God. The Father called sinners out of the darkness of sin and fitted them for the work of His kingdom. Christ purchased the church with His own blood. He is the head of the church, and the head of the church mediates His authority through His Word. And through the Word, the Holy Spirit does His work of sanctification in every believer's life. The Trinity speaks to the church, accomplishing the work of redemption through the Scripture.

How does the inerrancy of God's Word affect believers in terms of everyday life? Why should it matter to laypeople in the pew? Simply put, biblical authority is the bedrock of gospel truth. Once that is established, Scripture goes on to touch every aspect of the lives of the people of God, the church of the Lord Jesus. It defines everything regarding the work of God's kingdom. And as the state of the modern church illustrates, if we're not grounded in a right view of God's Word, there is no way to advance the kingdom.

Scripture is its own greatest defender, and no other work gives as clear and concise a testimony to Scripture's veracity, inerrancy, and authority. Perhaps no other passage of Scripture is more helpful in encouraging a commitment to the Word of God than Psalm 19. As we shall see, it is a rich treasure of truth about the Scripture.

# Creation Sings

The first six verses of Psalm 19 extol the glories of God's creative work.

> The heavens are telling of the glory of God;
> And their expanse is declaring the work of His hands.
> Day to day pours forth speech,
> And night to night reveals knowledge.
> There is no speech, nor are there words;
> Their voice is not heard.
> Their line has gone out through all the earth,
> And their utterances to the end of the world.
> In them He has placed a tent for the sun,
> Which is as a bridegroom coming out of his chamber;
> It rejoices as a strong man to run his course.
> Its rising is from one end of the heavens,
> And its circuit to the other end of them;
> And there is nothing hidden from its heat.
> (Ps. 19:1–6)

Creation loudly proclaims the power and majesty of the Creator. Theologians refer to the testimony of God in creation as general revelation. Through His creative work, God has put Himself on display so that all can see. The world and all that is in it reveal His glory. And David wants us to see that. He wants us to know that "the heavens are telling of the glory of God" (v. 1). All of creation points to its Creator, but here David chooses to emphasize the macro-creation that he knows no one can overlook. In fact, he takes that which is most obvious to every human who has ever lived—the heavenly bodies, and in particular, the sun.

In a sense, the sun is the focal point of human existence. It defines our days, shapes our seasons, and makes our planet habitable and fertile. It does all that as it hurtles through space at a half-million miles per hour, dragging our entire solar system around the galaxy. Scientists now know what the ancients could not—that the sun is a ball of nuclear fusion, twenty-eight million degrees Fahrenheit at its core. David draws our attention to the sun because it unmistakably points to the power and creativity of God's design—more than ever before, we know that the sun reveals the glory of the One who created it.

This revelation of God in His world is called "general" in the sense that it's available to all. In fact, as Paul explains in Romans 1, God's general revelation leaves those who rebelliously deny His existence without excuse (Rom. 1:18–20). That's the point behind David's scathing rebuke, "The fool has said in his heart, 'There is no God'" (Ps. 14:1). Only a fool would deny what the sun and the heavenly bodies tell us about their Creator.

## God's All-Sufficient Word

By contrast, the second half of Psalm 19 focuses entirely on *special* revelation, which is the revelation of God written in the Scriptures. Regarding what God has revealed about Himself in the pages of His Word, David writes the following:

The law of the LORD is perfect, restoring the soul;
The testimony of the LORD is sure, making wise the
  simple.
The precepts of the LORD are right, rejoicing the heart;
The commandment of the LORD is pure, enlightening
  the eyes.
The fear of the LORD is clean, enduring forever;
The judgments of the LORD are true; they are righteous
  altogether.
They are more desirable than gold, yes, than much
  fine gold;
Sweeter also than honey and the drippings of the
  honeycomb.
Moreover, by them Your servant is warned;
In keeping them there is great reward.
Who can discern his errors? Acquit me of hidden faults.
Also keep back Your servant from presumptuous sins;
Let them not rule over me;
Then I will be blameless,
And I shall be acquitted of great transgression.
Let the words of my mouth and the meditation of my
  heart

Be acceptable in Your sight,
O LORD, my rock and my Redeemer.
(Ps. 19:7–14)

There is no more concise tribute to the range of the authority of Scripture than this text. God, employing an economy of words through David's mind and pen, says all that must be said to encompass the length, breadth, depth, and height of Scripture's sufficiency.

If you serve in the church long enough, you'll see the Bible assaulted from virtually all sides. We've already mentioned the frontal attacks on its inspiration and inerrancy. In more recent years, there has been a rear assault from the experientialists who say, "Yes, the Bible is true, but so are my visions, dreams, and private revelations." While seemingly more benign, this viewpoint attacks the singularity of the faith once for all delivered to the saints (Jude 3). Scripture has also had to withstand side attacks from those who argue, "The Bible is certainly true, and it is the Word of God. But it lacks contemporary psychological and sociological sophistication, and therefore it suffers from relevance problems." In every instance, the debate boils down to the authority and sufficiency of Scripture. Does it really cover everything? Is it really all we need? Psalm 19 addresses these profound questions head-on.

Verses 7–9 highlight six essential truths about Scripture, along with their corresponding effect on the people of God. David uses six different words to describe Scripture, but each acknowledges God as the source through the repeated phrase,

"Of the LORD." The point of that repetition is emphasis—David is undeniably identifying Scripture as the Word of God.

## Internal Transformation

David first declares, "The law of the LORD is perfect, restoring the soul" (Ps. 19:7). Scripture is law. It is written by God as a manual for man's life. It is the manufacturer's manual for thought and behavior. God designed us, made us, and laid down the laws of operation for maximum benefit and blessing. The Bible is God's law for man, and it is perfect. Perfection refers not to the opposite of imperfection but to the opposite of incompletion. This is to say, the Bible is everything it needs to be. It lacks nothing. It is a flawless, perfectly sufficient revelation containing all that humanity requires to know the character and the will of God. In other words, the Bible is comprehensive and complete, lacking nothing related to man's knowledge of God and His law.

David tells us that this comprehensive Word restores the soul. The Hebrew word *nephesh* is translated "soul" in English versions today, but it can be translated more than twenty different ways, including "spirit," "being," "heart," and "self." But while many English words are used to translate *nephesh,* in the Hebrew it always means the same thing: the inner person and eternal being (as opposed to the body). God's Word is comprehensive, and it can restore the inner being of man. Scripture is not intended to create a superficial social morality or to fix the temporal issues of human existence. The Word of God is targeted specifically at restoring the immaterial person.

And what is meant by the word "restore"? It can mean "to renew," but the best translation is "to transform." The Word of God is so comprehensive, it can totally transform the whole inner person. That's what Scripture claims for itself. This is why Peter says, "For you have been born again . . . through the living and enduring word of God" (1 Peter 1:23). The Word convicts, penetrates, regenerates, and transforms. The writer of Hebrews says that it is "sharper than any two-edged sword, and piercing as far as the division of soul and spirit, of both joints and marrow, and able to judge the thoughts and intentions of the heart" (Heb. 4:12). It's not the skill of the preacher or a clever strategy that awakens cold, dead hearts. Scripture alone cuts to the core of the soul to convict and transform. That's the sufficient power of the Word to bring salvation and sanctification.

Some years ago, I was preaching in Florida. After one of the messages, a man approached me and said that he was a fifth-generation Jehovah's Witness. His father was in charge of the Jehovah's Witnesses movement in Florida, and this man worked to train their local leaders. While driving, he heard me on the radio, preaching that Jesus is God. He immediately turned it off but, out of curiosity, turned it back on and listened every day that week.

While traveling to train the local leadership of the Jehovah's Witnesses, he was in a motel and looked up to God and said, "If you, Jehovah, indeed came into this world in the form of Jesus Christ, if that's really true, would you let the light break on my heart?" By morning, he had repented and come to faith in Jesus Christ. Within six months, his father, mother, wife, and three sons—all Jehovah's Witnesses—were saved.

How do you reach a trainer embedded in the Jehovah's Witnesses? Do you need to be clever, to use the latest techniques? No; proclaim from the Scriptures that Jesus is God. God works through His Word.

A Jewish man called my church office, desperate to meet with me. He had been attending our church for four weeks. After listening to the preaching of the Word in a series titled *Delivered to Satan*, he said: "You were talking about me. I know I'm damned. I am an abortionist, and I kill babies for a living. Last year, my clinic did $9 million worth of abortions. If a woman doesn't have a reason, I give her one to get her money. Furthermore," he continued, "I divorced my wife, married my second wife, and now I'm living with a woman who is not my wife. I've been under psychiatric care for a year, and I'm facing bankruptcy. Can you help me?"

I told him that I was unable to help him, but that I knew someone who could transform his life—Jesus Christ. I told him to read from the gospel of John every day and to call me when he knew who Jesus was. Four days later, he returned and told me, "Jesus is God." This was a fifty-year-old man who had spent his whole life in Judaism. He said, "He has to be God because nobody could do what He did or say what He said if He wasn't God." He was speaking back to me exactly what John's gospel says. By the power of the Spirit of God, he understood. Not only that, but he had also found and read the book of Romans. Through the reading of the Word, his sin was laid bare before him, and he had been brought face-to-face with the Lord Jesus Christ. He told me he had written his resignation letter to the abortion clinic, and his wife was meeting him for church. Clearly, Scripture had dramatically affected him.

## Walking in Wisdom

In a sense, the power of Scripture is the most crucial truth that needs to be declared. But David continues extolling the character of God's Word. The second half of Psalm 19:7 reads, "The testimony of the LORD is sure, making wise the simple." Scripture is God's own self-revelation and testimony to who He is, and as such, it is sure. In a world full of unreliability, it is steadfast. In a world of lies and deceptions, it is trustworthy. This trustworthy self-revelation of God takes simple people and makes them wise. The Hebrew word translated "wisdom" is not similar to *sophia* in the Greek, which often refers to ethereal, intellectual wisdom. Instead, the Hebrew word *hokmah* speaks to wisdom in terms of skillful living. It's the ability to navigate life in this world in a God-honoring way. That's the kind of wisdom Scripture imparts to God's transformed people.

That point is further emphasized in the reference to the "simple." The Hebrew word here refers to an open door. In the Hebrew mind, a simple person was one who had an open mind. Today, it's considered a virtue for someone to say he has an open mind. But it is no virtue if you don't have the discernment to know what you should keep out and what you should keep in. David is describing someone who is unable to discriminate in the positive sense of the word. We have doors in our homes to keep some things out and other things in, and we open the doors at our discretion to make that distinction. In the same way, a wise man guards his mind. Only a fool would leave his mind open to anything and everything. But God's Word takes the naive, inexperienced, immature, uninformed, ignorant person whose mind is an open door and teaches him to be discerning.

Satan's primary tool is deception. He twists the meaning of Scripture. He establishes the man-centered religion of works (in all its various forms). And he dangles the false promise of satisfaction through temptation. Overcoming this onslaught of deception demands discernment. We have to have the wisdom to avoid deception and error; we have to know and live biblical truth. The psalmist makes that very point in Psalm 1: "How blessed is the man who does not walk in the counsel of the wicked, nor stand in the path of sinners, nor sit in the seat of scoffers! But his delight is in the law of the LORD, and in His law he meditates day and night. He will be like a tree firmly planted by streams of water, which yields its fruit in its season and its leaf does not wither; and in whatever he does, he prospers" (vv. 1–3). The Word of God makes the mind wise to withstand deception, able to navigate a holy life through this fallen world.

In just one verse, David has revealed that God's Word is capable of transforming the inner man (salvation) and of imparting the wisdom necessary to live a holy life (sanctification). There's more.

## The Only Path to Joy

In Psalm 19:8, David writes, "The precepts of the LORD are right, rejoicing the heart." This is looking at Scripture from the perspective of doctrine. God didn't merely give us His suggestions or some ideas we might want to try. These aren't ethereal truths that become real to us through existential experience. God's Word is absolute truth. Precepts or doctrines are divine principles, fixed statutes, and eternal propositional truths for the Christian life. Scripture supplies us with sound doctrine—it lays out the way God wants us to live. We're not meant to wander this dark, confused world with all its pitfalls and snares. God's Word gives us a right way to think and a right way to walk in the midst of the chaotic rebellion that surrounds us. This is a consistent theme in the Psalms. Psalm 119:105 says, "Your word is a lamp to my feet and a light to my path." God's Word gives us both the path to walk and the light we need to follow it.

And the fruit of following that path is a rejoicing heart. John writes in his first epistle, "These things we write, so that our joy may be made complete" (1 John 1:4). Full joy is directly linked to obedience to the truth. Jesus says, "Blessed are those who hear the word of God and observe it" (Luke 11:28). True joy comes from hearing, believing, and living the truth.

The prophet Jeremiah was hated throughout Israel because he preached repentance. Eventually, the Jews threw him into a pit so that they wouldn't have to hear his message any longer. But even at the lowest points in his ministry, when no one would listen and he had been rejected by everyone, this was Jeremiah's testimony: "Your words were found and I ate them, and Your words became for me a joy and the delight of my heart" (Jer. 15:16). If no one ever listened, paid any attention, or cared whatsoever, Jeremiah still had joy in the Word of God.

Faithfully following the path laid out for us in Scripture produces joy. It guides our lives and guards our steps, leading us in the path of joy and blessing. As Paul writes, "Let the word of Christ richly dwell within you, with all wisdom teaching and admonishing one another with psalms and hymns and spiritual songs, singing with thankfulness in your hearts to God" (Col. 3:16).

# True Enlightenment

Psalm 19:8 gives us another rich perspective on Scripture: "The commandment of the LORD is pure, enlightening the eyes." Here David is referring to God's divine decrees and mandates. These commandments are His sovereign, binding, nonnegotiable demands for His people. His Word is the authority over our very lives.

But "pure" is not the best translation for the word David employs to describe God's commandments. The better choice is "clear." He's describing the perspicuity of Scripture—it is lucid and transparent. There are people who would like us to think the Bible is dark, complicated, and mysterious, that its meaning is known only to the elite spiritual minds. Others think everyone has the freedom to interpret it any way they choose. David's point is just the opposite: God's Word is clear, exact, and singular in meaning, and it enlightens our eyes in this world filled with darkness.

Believers who grasp the truth of the Bible are the only people in the world who see things the way they really are. "We have the mind of Christ" (1 Cor. 2:16). We see the world for exactly what it is because we see it biblically. We understand life and death. We understand the origin of all things and the end that all things are marching toward. We can see the purposes of God unfolding throughout history. We understand good and evil, sin and righteousness. We understand how the Lord has ordered the world—how He restrains sinners and how His law works in the heart through the conscience. We understand the role of the family, the role of government, and what happens to a society when family and government start to break down. We understand the function of the church, the power of the gospel, and the work of the kingdom that God has called us to do. From the doctrines of God's Word, we understand reality with a clarity and perspective that unrepentant sinners could never comprehend.

I know a faithful missionary family serving the Lord in Utah, giving the gospel to Mormons. They came on a vacation to Southern California with their two daughters, one son, and an Italian exchange student they wanted to reach with the gospel. The trip included a Sunday visit to our church, as well as enrolling their daughter in The Master's University. As they were leaving Master's one afternoon and driving through an intersection, a truck ran a red light and hit their van. The collision instantly killed their two daughters and put their son and the exchange student in intensive care.

I was hoping to offer the parents some comfort in the midst

of that horrific event. As I began to speak to the husband, I asked him, "What's going through your mind right now?" He said: "My first thought is that this didn't happen—that it's all a dream. But I know that's not true." Then he said, "My second thought is this: Isn't God gracious, that He spared those two unconverted boys and took my two redeemed daughters that know Him?" That is clarity in the darkness that only God's Word can provide. Of course those parents' hearts were broken. But their broken hearts radiated with the love of their Savior and the hope of heaven. Without the Word, that kind of hope in the darkness is impossible. God's Word enlightens the eyes.

## Enduring Praise

David begins verse 9 of Psalm 19 with a fifth statement about the character of Scripture. He writes, "The fear of the LORD is clean, enduring forever." The fear of the Lord refers to respect, reverence, awe, and worship. David is talking about our praise to the Lord and is identifying Scripture as the divine manual for worship. Consider this: without God's Word, you wouldn't know the first thing about how to praise Him. The Lord Himself instructed us to worship Him "in spirit and truth" (John 4:24). Proverbs 9:10 tells us, "The fear of the LORD is the beginning of wisdom." Everything about the Christian life starts with true worship of God.

Not only has God given us His holy Word as the manual for worshiping Him, but David also adds that it's "clean."

It is free from error and corruption. This is a singular statement on the inerrancy of the Bible. It is totally untouched by defilement, impurity, or imperfection. The Psalms repeatedly emphasize this point; Psalm 12:6 says, "The words of the Lord are pure words; as silver tried in a furnace on the earth, refined seven times." The result of that purity is that His Word endures forever.

I remember having a discussion with some leaders from the so-called evangelical homosexual church. We were talking about the unmistakably clear fact that Scripture identifies homosexuality as sin. Their rebuttal was that the Bible is not always true because it is sociologically unsophisticated and antiquated—it doesn't take into consideration the full development of the potential for human relationships. Ultimately, they said, the Bible is an ancient book, and as such, it is irrelevant with regard to modern social issues.

My response was direct and to the point. Scripture's own testimony is that it is without error and, therefore, eternal. Christ testified that "not the smallest letter or stroke shall pass from the Law until all is accomplished" (Matt. 5:18). God's Word is not up for review, debate, or editing. In the words of the psalmist, "Forever, O Lord, Your word is settled in heaven" (Ps. 119:89). Scripture doesn't pass away, go out of date, or drift out of relevance. No one has the right to redact it, question its pertinence, or set it aside in favor of something more culturally sensitive or socially acceptable. It is flawless and perpetually true and thus the source of all praise and honor given to the Lord.

## Righteous Verdicts

Finally, David concludes this precise outline on the nature of God's Word with these words: "The judgments of the LORD are true; they are righteous altogether" (Ps. 19:9). The word "judgments" has to do with adjudications in a legal environment. Here, it refers to rulings from the divine Judge of all the earth, who renders the verdict on all people. Scripture contains God's verdicts as the One who alone holds all created beings under His absolute and righteous authority.

David says submitting to God's righteous judgments produces righteousness in us. There is no way to live a blessed life if we fundamentally disagree with God. Conversely, submitting to God's standard is the only way to cultivate a life of comprehensive righteousness. Left to ourselves, the best we can manage is temporary behavior modification and pharisaical self-righteousness that does not save us from His final verdict of eternal wrath.

For proof, look no further than the relativistic world around us. When everyone does what is right in his own eyes, it is a recipe for lawlessness, rebellion, and corruption. People are more than happy to talk about "their truth" and their self-made morality. But they can't stand the idea that God's Word is universally, absolutely, and objectively true. And they've been raised with a worldview that can't tolerate God or the Bible.

That's consistent with how Paul describes the spiritual warfare we're engaged in with the world: "For though we walk in the flesh, we do not war according to the flesh" (2 Cor. 10:3). Though we're human, we don't use human means—we don't go to war armed with marketing techniques or oratorical skills. "The weapons of our warfare," Paul says in verse 4, "are not of the flesh, but divinely powerful for the destruction of fortresses." We're assaulting the strongholds of Satan, and we need something more powerful than feeble, fleshly weapons if we intend to make an eternal impact. And what are those fortresses? He defines them in verse 5 as "speculations." The Greek word is *logismos*. It means ideologies, concepts, theories, philosophies, psychologies, and religions. We're attacking every false belief "and every lofty thing raised up against the knowledge of God, and we are taking every thought captive to the obedience of Christ" (v. 5).

We've been called into battle against every unbiblical, anti-God, anti-Christ ideology. The world is filled with false ideological fortresses void of truth that can't produce true righteousness or peace with God, and sinners are imprisoned within them. We assault those fortresses to lead prisoners out and bring their every thought captive to Jesus Christ. That's what evangelism is. Truth is the only weapon in our war against error. And the Bible is the only source for that truth that delivers from sin's prison.

## A Fitting Response

The final portions of Psalm 19 describe David's response to the six glorious facets of God's Word. If the law of the Lord can completely and eternally transform the whole inner person, make the simple person wise, bring true and lasting joy to the heart, make dark things clear, be permanently relevant, and produce true and complete righteousness, it is certainly "more desirable than gold, yes, than much fine gold; sweeter also than honey and the drippings of the honeycomb" (v. 10). The Word is our greatest possession and our greatest pleasure.

Verse 11 tells us that the Scriptures are also our greatest protection: "Moreover, by them Your servant is warned." God's Word guards us from sin and corruption. It points us to the way of escape, so we can withstand temptation (1 Cor. 10:13). The Scriptures are also our greatest provider, for "in keeping them there is great reward" (Ps. 19:11). On this side of eternity, there is no blessing more enriching than growing in our love for the Lord and our knowledge of His character. And there is no way to do that apart from His Word. We should echo the words of Job, who said, "I have treasured the words of His mouth more than my necessary food" (Job 23:12).

Finally, the Word of God is our greatest purifier. "Who can discern his errors? Acquit me of hidden faults. Also keep back Your servant from presumptuous sins; let them not rule over me; then I will be blameless, and I shall be acquitted of great transgression" (Ps. 19:12–13). God's Word reveals unchecked sin to us. It humbles us before the Lord, mortifies the habits of the flesh, and frees us from the bonds of sin and corruption. Without the purifying influence of Scripture, we would easily wander into apostasy. As the psalmist wrote in Psalm 119:11, "Your word I have treasured in my heart, that I may not sin against You."

David closes Psalm 19 with a prayerful reflection: "Let the words of my mouth and the meditation of my heart be acceptable in Your sight, O LORD, my rock and my Redeemer" (Ps. 19:14). It's likely that this is a reference by David to Joshua 1:8, which says, "This book of the law shall not depart from your mouth, but you shall meditate on it day and night, so that you may be careful to do according to all that is written in it; for then you will make your way prosperous, and then you will have success."

If we desire a meditation that pleases God, we must meditate on Scripture. If we want to speak words that please Him, we must speak the words of Scripture. The words of our mouths should be the words of God, and the meditations of our hearts should be divine truth. That's the only appropriate response to the authority of God's Word. That is the essence of worship.

## Chapter Four

# THE BIBLE IS THE CATALYST OF SPIRITUAL GROWTH

G od's Word is the priority in spiritual growth. It's the Holy Spirit's tool and the believer's food; therefore, it's the means of sanctification. All the other means of grace flow to us out of Scripture. As we saw in Psalm 19, it is vital to our salvation, and it sets the foundation for the life of faith.

One of the most remarkable statements that Jesus ever made occurs in His High Priestly Prayer in John 17. In the Greek, it's three words: *egō hagiazō emauton*. In English, "I sanctify Myself" (John 17:19). This is a stunning statement from a human perspective, and it is made not to people but to God, without a hint of hesitation.

We know that to be sanctified is to be separated from sin. Scripture says of Jesus that He was "holy, innocent, undefiled, separated from sinners" (Heb. 7:26). But the wonder of this statement is that He sanctified *Himself*. The verb tense indicates continuity: in other words, He is always sanctifying Himself. He constantly separates Himself from sin and sustains His own holiness, though tempted relentlessly at all points, as we are (Heb. 4:15).

Praying for His followers in John 17:17, Jesus says, "Sanctify them in the truth; Your word is truth." And then in verse 19, "For their sakes I sanctify Myself, that they themselves also may be sanctified in truth." In both instances in verse 17, as well as in verse 19, He uses the word *alētheia* for "truth." We are sanctified in the truth, and He sanctifies Himself that we may also be sanctified in truth. This is the ultimate key to spiritual growth—to be separated from sin and joined in knowledge and obedience to the Word of God.

## A Testimony of Obedience

Perfect obedience to the will and Word of God is demonstrated in the life of the Son of God. In John 4:34, He says, "My food is to do the will of Him who sent Me and to accomplish His work." In John 5:19, He says, "Truly, truly, I say to you, the Son can do nothing of Himself, unless it is something He sees the Father doing; for whatever the Father does, these things the Son also does in like manner." In verse 30 of the same chapter, He states: "I can do nothing on My own initiative. As I hear, I judge; and My judgment is just, because I do not seek My own will, but the will of Him who sent Me." This is perfect sanctification—to consistently and comprehensively submit to the will of God.

In John 6:38, He proclaims, "For I have come down from heaven, not to do My own will, but the will of Him who sent Me." In John 7:18, we read, "He who speaks from himself seeks his own glory; but He who is seeking the glory of the One who sent Him, He is true, and there is no unrighteousness in Him." It is by seeking the glory of God, obeying the truth of God, and pursuing the will of God that one is sanctified. He goes on in John 8:28, "When you lift up the Son of Man, then you will know that I am He, and I do nothing on My own initiative, but I speak these things as the Father taught Me." And then a key statement in verse 29: "For I always do the things that are pleasing to Him." Fundamental to Christ's self-sanctification was His perfect obedience to the will of God. As He says in John 14:31, "So that the world may know that I love the Father, I do exactly as the Father commanded Me." And when He was tempted, how did He respond? He used the book of Deuteronomy, defending Himself against the deceptions of Satan and answering every temptation with an affirmation of the truth and revelation of God (Luke 4:1–13).

"I sanctify Myself," He prayed, with no fear of rebuttal on the part of His omniscient and holy Father, who Himself declared, "This is My beloved Son, in whom I am well-pleased" (Matt. 3:17).

## Scripture-Driven Spiritual Growth

Christ's life gives us an example of perfect sanctification through His sinlessness and flawless obedience to His Father. Obviously, we will never know that kind of perfect righteousness on this side of heaven. Still, it is our model of the life that honors God.

In fact, that which set Christ apart to God is exactly what sets the believer apart. Christ's own personal testimony to His sanctification is part of a prayer that embraced all of us: "Sanctify them in the truth; Your word is truth" (John 17:17). Scripture is the source of all sanctifying truth. All other gracious means of sanctification are necessarily revealed to us in God's Word, so that is where we must start.

As Paul says to Timothy in his second letter, "From childhood you have known the sacred writings which are able to give you the wisdom that leads to salvation through faith which is in Christ Jesus" (2 Tim. 3:15). The Apostle John, writing under the inspiration of the Holy Spirit, understood well the role that the truth plays in sanctification, as we see throughout his brief epistles. In 2 John, he writes the following:

> The elder to the chosen lady and her children, whom I love in truth; and not only I, but also all who know the truth, for the sake of the truth which abides in us and will be with us forever: Grace, mercy and peace will be with us, from God the Father and from Jesus Christ, the Son of the Father, in truth and love. I was very glad to find some of your children walking in truth, just as we have received commandment to do from the Father. (vv. 1–4)

Five times in this salutation, the word *alētheia* (truth) appears. John knew that sanctification comes only by the truth.

He desired to find the people under his pastoral care walking in the truth, and he rejoiced when they did, because that's the path of spiritual growth. In his first epistle, John says, "Whoever keeps His word, in him the love of God has truly been perfected" (1 John 2:5). God's redeeming, saving love is perfected in the person who fully obeys His truth. John continues: "By this we know that we are in Him: the one who says he abides in Him ought himself to walk in the same manner as He walked" (vv. 5–6). True believers must walk as Christ walked. The claim of belonging to God and being a child of God ought to be evidenced in faithfully living out the truth, just as Jesus did. He kept the Father's Word perfectly. Believers who abide in Him will not experience perfection in this life, but the pursuit of holiness and biblical fidelity will be the clear trajectory of their lives.

The Apostle John had more to say about protecting our spiritual growth. In his second epistle, he writes: "This is love, that we walk according to His commandments. This is the commandment, just as you have heard from the beginning, that you should walk in it. For many deceivers have gone out into the world, those who do not acknowledge Jesus Christ as coming in the flesh. This is the deceiver and the antichrist. Watch yourselves, that you do not lose what we have accomplished, but that you may receive a full reward" (2 John 6–8). The believer's spiritual growth yields an ever-increasing weight of glory, which can be forfeited by distraction from the truth into deception and sin. This affects not only the here and now, harming the believer's spiritual development, usefulness, and joy; but it also has a lasting effect, including the potential loss of eternal reward.

In fact, we are warned that if anyone comes along who does not abide in the true teaching concerning Christ, we should not let him into our house or give him a greeting, lest we become partakers "in his evil deeds" (vv. 10–11). From beginning to end, the Bible contains similar warnings to stay away from false teaching, because anything that corrupts our understanding of the truth halts sanctification, which inhibits our usefulness to God's kingdom.

John's third epistle further emphasizes the Apostle's preoccupation with this necessary foundation of spiritual growth. "To the beloved Gaius," he writes, "whom I love in truth. . . . I was very glad when brethren came and testified to your truth, that is, how you are walking in truth. I have no greater joy than this, to hear of my children walking in the truth" (3 John 1, 3–4). In verse 8, he continues, "We ought to support such men, so that we may be fellow workers with the truth." And in verse 12, he commends a man named Demetrius, who "received a good testimony from everyone, and from the truth itself; and we add our testimony, and you know that our testimony is true." In other words, Demetrius was consistent with revealed truth. These two little postcard epistles call us to a simple but clear understanding that the foundation of all spiritual growth and godliness is divine truth.

Jude, an epistle hidden in the shadow of Revelation, should never be overlooked. In verse 3, Jude says, "Beloved, while I was making every effort to write you about our common salvation. . . ." That is a fascinating statement. Have you ever tried to write a letter you couldn't write or to communicate a message you simply couldn't get out of your mouth? As a pastor, there have been many times I have started a sermon that I couldn't finish because my heart was burdened and directed in another way. And so it was with Jude.

In spite of his initial intentions, he writes, "I felt the necessity to write to you appealing that you contend earnestly for the faith which was once for all handed down to the saints" (v. 3). Jude is saying that if we do not faithfully battle to protect the truth, there won't be a common salvation or common gospel to celebrate. He was concerned not that his readers would lose their faith but that the emergence of false teachers would inhibit the evangelistic progress of the true gospel. He was troubled at the prospect of these apostate apostles leading lost sinners further away from the truth and into greater confusion and error. The corrupting influence of false teaching moves rapidly, and Jude wanted to stifle its progress as soon as possible.

How could the faith be protected and preserved? Jude gives us his prescription: "But you, beloved, ought to remember the words that were spoken beforehand by the apostles of our Lord Jesus Christ" (v. 17), exhorting his readers again, "But you, beloved, [build] yourselves up on your most holy faith, praying in the Holy Spirit" (v. 20).

These epistles all agree that the primary instrument of our spiritual growth is Scripture. It is the truth that saves. It is the truth that sanctifies. It is the truth that makes us wise unto salvation. And it is the truth that refines and purifies us, thoroughly equipping us for all good works. All spiritual work is the work of God's Word in the power of God's Spirit.

The obvious implications of this are startling. The more that God's truth is removed from our lives, the more inhibited our spiritual progress becomes. Nothing else can do the work that the truth does. There is no sanctifying power in human wisdom, intuition, insight, or experience. It is only in the Word of God. Only the truth revealed in Scripture sanctifies—sound teaching accurately interpreted, understood, and applied. As divine revelation is embraced, spiritual progress is made. There are no alternate routes to godly character and holy living.

## The Stages of Sanctification

There's more for us to glean from the Apostle John regarding the role of the Word in our spiritual growth. His first epistle contains a definitive paradigm for sanctification, matchless among the texts of the New Testament. He writes:

> I am writing to you, little children, because your sins have been forgiven you for His name's sake. I am writing to you, fathers, because you know Him who has been from the beginning. I am writing to you, young men, because you have overcome the evil one. I have written to you, children, because you know the Father. I have written to you, fathers, because you know Him who has been from the beginning. I have written to you, young men, because you are strong, and the word

of God abides in you, and you have overcome the evil one. (1 John 2:12–14)

In the opening statement of verse 12, John calls the recipients of his letter "little children." The Greek word translated here, *teknia*, refers not to children in terms of age but to offspring in a general sense. John is writing generally to all of God's children, all of the regenerate, redeemed, and justified. But in verses 13–14, he places believers into three spiritual groups: fathers, young men, and children. With these designations, he is characterizing believers according to three different stages of spiritual growth.

## Children

Verse 13 begins with "children." John uses a different Greek word here than the one he uses in verse 12; here, it is *paideia*. This word refers to children under pedagogical training, those in the earliest formative years, who still require elemental instruction. John is describing young children who are ignorant and immature, who need discipline, control, and guidance. This is what it means to be a spiritual child—not in the general sense of being a child of God but rather simply being childish in nature.

And what is characteristic of a spiritual child? John says, "You know the Father." At this stage of development, there is parental recognition—as Paul says, "We cry out, 'Abba! Father!'" (Rom. 8:15). The immature child in John's analogy is attached to mother and father, and the bond is strong. Parental recognition dominates his life. He is dependent, and he is influenced more by trust than by understanding.

However, this stage is not meant to be permanent. As Paul explains to the believers in Ephesus, "We are no longer to be children, tossed here and there by waves and carried about by every wind of doctrine, by the trickery of men, by craftiness in deceitful scheming" (Eph. 4:14). To be a spiritual child is to be vulnerable, weak, and undiscerning. It means one is still unable to plumb the depths of God's Word or feast on the rich meat of His truth. In some ways, it is a very dangerous place to be; with spiritual children, there is often a broad sense of tolerance but not the will or the means to discriminate carefully. This is why the Lord gave pastors and teachers to the church, so that all might grow out of this childish stage and into the full stature of Christlikeness. As Paul charges the Ephesians, by "speaking the truth in love, we are to grow up in all aspects into Him who is the head, even Christ" (v. 15).

Much—if not most—of the evangelical church today falls into this category. They rejoice in the simplicity of their attachment to the Father. They sing repetitive worship choruses celebrating their dependence on God, but they really have no love for the rich theology of hymns, nor the will to discern or distinguish truth from falsehood, nor the means by which to do so. They're absorbed with feelings, preoccupied by temporal concerns, and susceptible to worldly temptations. This stage has nothing to do with how long one has been a Christian; it has to do with how much sound doctrine has taken over one's thinking. Tragically, churches cater to people stuck in this infantile stage, operating as though it is an acceptable, permanent level of spiritual development.

This initial stage of spiritual growth isn't in itself negative, because it is normal. New believers' lives are marked by exuberant love for the Lord and the sincere desire to praise Him and to hear His Word. But through our ongoing exposure to that Word, the Lord means to grow us out of that early stage of spiritual childhood into spiritual adulthood. True believers must not be content to stay in the shallows of spiritual immaturity. And true churches must not encourage or enable such spiritual stasis.

## Young Men

The Apostle's second category of spiritual growth is "young men." John says they have "overcome the evil one" (1 John 2:13). That is a powerful reality. Verse 14 adds that this power over Satan is attained because these believers are "strong," because "the word of God abides" in them, and again because such Christians "have overcome the evil one." What is the difference between a spiritual child and a spiritual young man? In a word: strength. In particular, it's the strength that comes from the knowledge of the Word of God. The word translated here as "young men" is the word for "youth"—it can also mean "strong" or "mature." They are characterized as having the Word of God abiding in them; therefore, they are strong in the truth.

I see this strength frequently in my own pastoral work,

and particularly with young men at The Master's Seminary. I watch them go from a loving relationship to God and an overwhelming sense of being attached to Him as their loving Father to the maturity that comes as they progress in knowing and understanding doctrine. They go from being weak and needing protection to being strong and ready to fight for the truth. You can mark them out because they want to go to battle with error. They want to expose false teaching. They no longer want to talk only of the basics of Christian life. They want to learn to answer all the doctrinal questions and to understand all the features of theology, developing spiritual muscle from this pursuit.

And the amazing benefit of progressing to this stage is overcoming the evil one. John says it twice: "You have overcome the evil one." He describes it in the past tense with continuing results. This ongoing victory over the ancient, clever, and deceptive Satan sounds like an overstatement. What can John mean?

The word translated "overcome" is the Greek *nikaō*. It means to "conquer," "prevail," or "win." Thus, John is clearly saying that believers strong in the doctrine of God's Word have, in some way, conquered and prevailed over Satan. We can grasp that sense as we know that "Satan disguises himself as an angel of light" (2 Cor. 11:14). His primary goal is to deceive and confuse—to corrupt minds, leading them away from the truth and the gospel into damning lies. When one is grounded in sound doctrine and strong in the truth of God's Word, he is not susceptible to those deceptions. That's the potent benefit of knowing the truth—we can discern the strategies and deceptions of Satan and not be "ignorant of his schemes" (2 Cor. 2:11).

Having said that, no one is perfect. Believers will fall into temptation, but those who are steeped in the truth are unlikely to be seduced into false doctrine. They do not become fearful or doubtful; they're not easily persuaded or deceived. Rather, they're rooted in the truth and strong in the faith. They storm the gates of falsehood, eager to assault Satan's ideological fortresses and defend the truth of Scripture, bringing "every thought captive to the obedience of Christ" (2 Cor. 10:5).

## Fathers

The ultimate level of spiritual development that John identifies—"fathers"—is the fullest and most joyful stage for those who walk with the Lord. He says, "I am writing to you, fathers, because you know Him who has been from the beginning" (1 John 2:13), repeating the same idea in verse 14. He's describing people who have progressed beyond knowing the truth about the Lord to truly knowing the Lord. It's the difference between knowing facts about God and actually knowing Him intimately. John is talking about believers who are enthralled with God, who live in the wonder, love, and praise of their heavenly Father—much as when they were first saved, but now with longer experiences of providence, answered prayer, deeper doctrine, and truth-loaded worship. There may be no more exemplary Christian than the Apostle Paul, and even he was anxious to keep growing in this regard.

Philippians 3:10 records the plea of his heart: "that I may know Him." The current knowledge of God is never enough.

For someone at this stage, the Lord is the object of his love, adoration, and delight. His biblical knowledge has introduced him to the Lord, and now he engages in communion with Him that has deepened throughout the years. He has watched the biblical realities that he knows to be true unfold in the marvelous providences of life. A person in this stage loves the Lord, and it is his life's passion to honor and glorify Him.

I have seen that reality in my own life. I have seen God's hand of providence working in the lives of my family members, redeeming my children and grandchildren. I've seen Him pour out boundless blessing and dole out chastisement when necessary. I've seen Him spare us in the face of severe illness and injury and shepherd our lives in countless providential ways. And as God's endearing care richly unfolds throughout life, it is no longer just about theology but about rich, intimate communion with Him.

It must grieve the Lord to see evangelical churches filled with people in spiritual infancy, robbed of the richness of biblical doctrine and a thorough, potent knowledge of God's Word. Worse still, they are cheated out of an intimate sense of His personal love and providential involvement in their lives, as all that is true about Him vividly unfolds before them. It shouldn't have to be said, but the church must not deny God's people the truth of His Word, stifling their growth and their usefulness to His kingdom.

The state of any church can be known clearly by the content

of the preaching, the gravity of the worship, and the doctrinal and God-centered nature of the music.

## The Means of Maturity

How do we advance through the stages of spiritual maturity? We don't want to remain spiritual children, perpetually stuck in infancy. We don't want to be weak, vulnerable, and immature. Nor do we want to be ignorant about God's truth, because we want to fully glorify Him for everything He has done. We want to appreciate Him in all His fullness, knowing and loving Him thoroughly. If that's the goal, then how do we get there? How do we respond to the Word in a way that drives that progress?

I see three definitive steps in the biblical pattern of sanctification. The first is *cognition*. John 17:17 gives our Lord's prayer: "Sanctify them in the truth; Your word is truth." We have to understand what the Bible says and what it means if it is going to produce growth in us. Sanctification begins with spiritually renewing the mind, that is, changing how we think. We need "the mind of Christ" (1 Cor. 2:16). There is no premium on ignorance or naivete in sanctification. The discipline of putting the truth constantly at the forefront of our minds is crucial.

If we lack spiritual maturity, we must read everything we can that faithfully and accurately explains the Word of God to us. We must study the Bible and memorize it; we must read commentaries from biblical scholars, listen to sermons from faithful expositors, and read the biographies of godly saints whose lives display the kind of maturity we want to see in our own lives. We must soak our minds in the Scriptures, fueling the Spirit's sanctifying work.

That seems like an obvious first step, but it's one that many believers fail to take. They can't fathom why they keep succumbing to the same temptations and why their love for the Lord has cooled and their interest in His church has plateaued. They fail to understand that the absence of biblical knowledge retards spiritual thinking and slows spiritual growth.

Don't confuse childlike faith with childish thinking. Legalism won't lead us to holiness and spiritual maturity. Mysticism and sacramentalism won't get us there, either. Pragmatism will likely lead us in the wrong direction, and it invites us to pursue quick fixes and worldly wisdom instead of grounding us in the truth of God's Word. The only activity that catalyzes the ongoing sanctifying process is taking in the truth of Scripture. Cognition—knowing and understanding the truth—is the first step in pursuing spiritual growth through the Word of God.

After cognition comes *conviction*. As we learn the truth of Scripture, we must begin to develop beliefs into convictions. Our lives are controlled by our convictions. As the truth of God's Word begins to occupy our minds and shape our thoughts, it will produce principles that we desire not to violate. This is what sanctification is about—being inwardly compelled to obedience.

The Apostle Paul suffered many things during his ministry—imprisonment, severe beatings, shipwrecks, and a constant stream of unfounded accusations from false teachers.

In 2 Corinthians 4, he describes the difficulties of his life: "We are afflicted in every way, but not crushed; perplexed, but not despairing; persecuted, but not forsaken; struck down, but not destroyed" (vv. 8–9). In verse 11, he continues, "For we who live are constantly being delivered over to death for Jesus' sake." Every day, he understood that any one of the several plots against him could come to fruition. At any moment, he could be dead. Everywhere he went, he offended people. He was constantly being thrown out of synagogues and into prison. He lived in a perpetual cycle of opposition and oppression.

What made him keep going in spite of all the hardship he faced? In verse 13, he quotes the Psalms, saying, "I believed, therefore I spoke." That is conviction. Paul might as well say: "What else do you want me to do? There is no alternative for me. This is my conviction from the Word of God."

That conviction shaped Paul's life and ministry. Earlier in 2 Corinthians, he testified, "For our proud confidence is this: the testimony of our conscience, that in holiness and godly sincerity, not in fleshly wisdom but in the grace of God, we have conducted ourselves in the world, and especially toward you" (1:12). Paul was true to the wisdom of God, and his conscience did not accuse him, regardless of the accusations against him. In Acts 23:1, he says, "Brethren, I have lived my life with a perfectly good conscience before God up to this day," and in Acts 24:16, "I also do my best to maintain always a blameless conscience both before God and before men." Paul's firm convictions, rooted in Scripture, helped him live a righteous life, with nothing to be ashamed of.

John Bunyan, the great Puritan preacher and author of *The Pilgrim's Progress*, remained in jail for twelve years, but it wasn't the prison bars that held him there. He could have walked free if he would simply promise to stop preaching. Facing that option, Bunyan wrote, "If nothing will do, unless I make of my conscience a continual butchery and slaughter-shop, unless putting out my own eyes I commit me to the blind to lead me, I have determined, the Almighty God being my help and shield, yet to suffer, if frail life might continue so long, even till the moss shall grow on mine eye-brows rather than thus to violate my faith and principles."[1] That is conviction. When we read the Bible, we are learning the Word of God in order to develop convictions that will rule our lives and hold our consciences captive, activating them when we start to violate God's righteous standard. Biblical truth establishes cognition in the mind and develops restraint in the conscience.

The third feature is *affection*. The love of God's truth is a consistent theme throughout Scripture, and particularly in the Psalms. Psalm 119 is an exhaustive account of the psalmist's love for the truth and his delight in the law. We've already looked at Psalm 19, where David says that God's Word is "more desirable than gold, yes, than much fine gold; sweeter also than honey and the drippings of the honeycomb" (v. 10). Or look at Psalm 1, which describes the great blessing for the one whose "delight is in the law of the LORD, and in His law he meditates day and night" (v. 2). As we expose ourselves to the Word, we begin to understand what it says. It begins to form our convictions, and then it becomes our sincere affection.

How strong should that affection be? Peter put it this way: "Like newborn babies, long for the pure milk of the word, so that by it you may grow in respect to salvation" (1 Peter 2:2). Spiritual growth comes when we know the Word, when it shapes our convictions, and when we learn to long for the sustenance it alone can provide.

Psalm 42:1 says, "As the deer pants for the water brooks, so my soul pants for You, O God." The psalmist is not referring to the way some people read the Bible as a curiosity or as ancient literature. He's not talking about perusing the Bible for intellectual stimulation or gathering ammunition to win an argument. This is studying Scripture eagerly and earnestly, hungry to extract all of the nourishment we so desperately need out of the Word.

The Word of God is our spiritual sustenance. May we have the same solitary longing for it that a baby has for milk—because by it, we are conformed to the image of Christ, who sanctified Himself for us. The Word reveals Christ to us, and the Word transforms us into His likeness. We are reminded of what our Savior repeated three times in the upper room—that He would send us the Holy Spirit. We know that sanctification is a divine work through the Word by the Spirit of truth. So, we must plead with the Spirit that He would mold and shape us into the image of Christ, through the truth, from one level of glory to the next. As the Apostle Paul explains, "But we all, with unveiled face, beholding as in a mirror the glory of the Lord, are being transformed into the same image from glory to glory, just as from the Lord, the Spirit" (2 Cor. 3:18).

## Chapter Five

# THE BIBLE IS CENTRAL TO FAITHFUL MINISTRY

"How can I find a good church in my area?" I hear that question often, as I meet Christians who keep striking out in their attempts to find a biblical congregation where they live. Often, these people are desperate to be faithfully fed the riches of God's Word. And while I'm encouraged by their hunger for the truth, I'm grieved that good churches are so scarce.

It is true, however, that people can be and often are their own greatest hindrances when it comes to finding a church. Some are too easily annoyed or offended by the preacher or the parking, or too quick to complain if the style of the service or the music doesn't fit their precise tastes. The problem isn't that they can't find a good church; the problem is that they're using the wrong criteria. They've elevated their tastes and preferences to the level of biblical mandates, and they won't settle for anything less.

In cases like this, the pivotal issue is often the perceived faults of the pastor. There seems to be no end to the reasons people will turn their backs on a preacher. Maybe they think he lacks personal magnetism, contemporary savvy, or a commanding presence. Maybe he didn't go to their preferred school, or he doesn't quote their favorite theologians. Maybe his sermons aren't engaging enough—maybe he needs to inject more humor and more stories into his preaching. Or maybe his sermons just need to be shorter. I've heard these and countless other excuses from believers explaining why they left their churches.

When I'm able, I try to remind those who are quick to complain that Scripture contains clear commands for the congregation, too. For example, 1 Thessalonians 5:12–13 says, "But we request of you, brethren, that you appreciate those who diligently labor among you, and have charge over you in the Lord and give you instruction, and that you esteem them very highly in love because of their work." In Hebrews 13:7, we read, "Remember those who led you, who spoke the word of God to you; and considering the result of their conduct, imitate their faith," and in verse 17: "Obey your leaders and submit to them, for they keep watch over your souls as those who will give an account. Let them do this with joy and not with grief, for this would be unprofitable for you." God's Word is clear: the people in the pews are to appreciate, esteem, love, imitate, obey, and submit to faithful, biblical leaders and not to cause them grief.

## The Marks of a Faithful Shepherd

The question, then, is what kind of leader is worthy of this type of respect? What kind of leader is worthy to be followed? While a noble minister of Jesus Christ embodies many traits, of critical importance is the pastor's commitment to giving His people the true Word of God. What are the distinguishing marks of a genuine shepherd of the Lord's flock? How are the people in the pews to identify a faithful pastor who will lead them in the knowledge of God?

For us to identify the biblical criteria, we need only look to the Apostle Paul and his divinely inspired charge to his young apprentice in the faith, Timothy.

In pointing out these things to the brethren, you will be a good servant of Christ Jesus, constantly nourished on the words of the faith and of the sound doctrine which you have been following. But have nothing to do with worldly fables fit only for old women. On the other hand, discipline yourself for the purpose of godliness; for bodily discipline is only of little profit, but godliness is profitable for all things, since it holds promise for the present life and also for the life to come. It is a trustworthy statement deserving full acceptance. For it is for this we labor and strive, because we have fixed our hope on the living God, who is the Savior of all men, especially of believers. Prescribe and teach these things. Let no one look down on your youthfulness, but rather in speech, conduct, love, faith and purity, show yourself an example of those who believe. Until I come, give attention to the public reading of Scripture, to exhortation and teaching. Do not neglect the spiritual gift within you, which was bestowed on you through prophetic utterance with the laying on of hands by the presbytery. Take pains with these things; be absorbed in them, so that your progress will be evident to all. Pay close attention to yourself and to your teaching; persevere in these things, for as you do this you will ensure salvation both for yourself and for those who hear you. (1 Tim. 4:6–16)

In these eleven verses, Paul gives us the criteria by which all pastors must be measured. For the purposes of this book, we're going to highlight the biblical qualities that directly pertain to the ministry of the Word.[1]

## Faithful to Protect

First, a godly minister of Christ Jesus will warn his people of error. First Timothy 4:6 says, "In pointing out these things to the brethren, you will be a good servant of Christ Jesus." To "point out" (Greek *hupotithemai*) basically means to "lay out" or "bring to one's attention." What is Timothy supposed to bring to the attention of the congregation? Paul established that in verses 1–3 of the same chapter: "In later times some will fall away from the faith, paying attention to deceitful spirits and doctrines of demons, by means of the hypocrisy of liars seared in their own conscience as with a branding iron, men who forbid marriage and advocate abstaining from foods which God has created to be gratefully shared in by those who believe and know the truth." Paul's desire is that Timothy—and all who shepherd the flock of God—would faithfully warn believers of false teachers, heresy, and demonic lies designed to draw them away from the truth.

This is not the first or the last time in these letters that the vital importance of guarding the flock from error will be addressed. First Timothy 1:3–4 says, "As I urged you upon my departure for Macedonia, remain on at Ephesus so that you may instruct certain men not to teach strange doctrines, nor to pay attention to myths and endless genealogies, which give rise to mere speculation rather than furthering the administration of God which is by faith." Verses 6–7 continue, "For some men, straying from these things, have turned aside to fruitless discussion, wanting to be teachers of the Law, even though they do not understand either what they are saying or the matters about which they make confident assertions." Some of the men seeking to influence people are even characterized by Paul as "unholy and profane" (v. 9).

He goes on to exhort Timothy in verses 18–20: "This command I entrust to you, Timothy, my son, in accordance with the prophecies previously made concerning you, that by them you fight the good fight, keeping faith and a good conscience, which some have rejected and suffered shipwreck in regard to their faith. Among these are Hymenaeus and Alexander, whom I have handed over to Satan, so that they will be taught not to blaspheme." The Apostle concludes his letter with a similar charge: "O Timothy, guard what has been entrusted to you, avoiding worldly and empty chatter and the opposing arguments of what is falsely called 'knowledge'— which some have professed and thus gone astray from the faith. Grace be with you" (6:20–21).

Paul issued a similar warning of such danger when he left the Ephesian church:

> I know that after my departure savage wolves will come in among you, not sparing the flock; and from among your own selves men will arise, speaking perverse things, to draw away the disciples after them. Therefore be on the alert, remembering that night and day for a period of three years I did not cease to admonish each one with tears. And now I commend you to God and to the word of His grace, which is able to build you up and to give you the inheritance among all those who are sanctified. (Acts 20:29–32)

Fidelity to the truth of Scripture and the protection of God's people were of paramount importance to Paul—and they must be to us, as well. Scripture makes clear that the defense of the truth is critical. In fact, it's woven into the biblical requirements for elders and pastors. Godly leaders must "[hold] fast the faithful word which is in accordance with the teaching, so that he will be able both to exhort in sound doctrine and to refute those who contradict. For there are many rebellious men, empty talkers and deceivers, especially those of the circumcision, who must be silenced because they are upsetting whole families, teaching things they should not teach for the sake of sordid gain" (Titus 1:9–11).

Much of the chaos and confusion in the church today is the direct result of pastors' failing to carefully discharge their duty to teach sound doctrine and train people to be discerning, so as to guard the church from error. That failure is the reason that so many professing believers think they should be looking for fresh revelation from God, why they're so eager to hear about the visions, dreams, and impressions of others while their Bibles sit closed on the pew next to them. It's the reason so many Christians have caved to worldly wisdom, allowing godless academics and skeptics to shape how we understand God's creative work and how we answer the onslaught of questions about gender, sex, and identity. The abdication of pastoral protection is why so many ecumenical endeavors have succeeded in sowing confusion within the church, blurring the lines between true faith in Christ and the various satanic substitutes. The list could go on and on, as there is no end to the horrors unleashed on the church by the false teaching of wolves, because shepherds fail to protect the flock of God.

A common defense among those who fail to warn their congregations is that "God hasn't called me to that kind of pastoral ministry." I'll submit to you that *there is no other kind of pastoral ministry*. A preacher is not faithful to his task if he fails to hold up the Word of God before his people in such a way that they can discern the truth from error. He's not really a pastor in the first place.

As a reminder of just how seriously God takes the protection of His people, consider His warning to the prophet Ezekiel:

Son of man, I have appointed you a watchman to the house of Israel; whenever you hear a word from My mouth, warn them from Me. When I say to the wicked, "You will surely die," and you do not warn him or speak out to warn the wicked from his wicked way that he may live, that wicked man shall die in his iniquity, but his blood I will require at your hand. Yet if you have warned the wicked and he does not turn from his wickedness or from his wicked way, he shall die in his iniquity; but you have delivered yourself. Again, when a righteous man turns away from his righteousness and commits iniquity, and I place an obstacle before him, he will die; since you have not warned him, he shall die in his sin, and his righteous deeds which he has done shall not be remembered; but his blood I will require at your hand. However, if you have warned the righteous man that the righteous should not sin and he does not sin, he shall surely live because he took warning; and you have delivered yourself. (Ezek. 3:17–21)

Christ echoed that warning with similar severity when He told His disciples, "Whoever causes one of these little ones who believe in Me to stumble, it would be better for him to have a heavy millstone hung around his neck, and to be drowned in the depth of the sea" (Matt. 18:6). Woe to those pastors who fail to protect God's people.

This notion may be unpopular, but it is crucial to shepherding the flock. We hear people sometimes say in defense of ministers who fail to be strong in Scripture and theology, "Well, he's got a pastor's heart." But a good shepherd is not known by how gently he pets the sheep. A good shepherd is known by how well he protects them and feeds them. Paul's closing charge in 2 Timothy makes the priority of this duty abundantly clear:

> I solemnly charge you in the presence of God and of Christ Jesus, who is to judge the living and the dead, and by His appearing and His kingdom: preach the word; be ready in season and out of season; reprove, rebuke, exhort, with great patience and instruction. For the time will come when they will not endure sound doctrine; but wanting to have their ears tickled, they will accumulate for themselves teachers in accordance to their own desires, and will turn away their ears from the truth and will turn aside to myths. But you, be sober in all things, endure hardship, do the work of an evangelist, fulfill your ministry. (2 Tim. 4:1–5)

## Faithful to Study

Second in Paul's list of criteria, the godly shepherd must also be a serious student of Scripture. First Timothy 4:6 speaks of Timothy's being "constantly nourished on the words of the faith and of the sound doctrine which you have been following." Paul knew that Timothy was already well versed in the truth. "From childhood you have known the sacred writings which are able to give you the wisdom that leads to salvation through faith which is in Christ Jesus" (2 Tim. 3:15). This is an exhortation to stay immersed in Scripture and faithful to its truth.

Being "constantly nourished" connotes a continual process of self-feeding on the Word of God. The godly pastor needs to hunger for the truth the way a hungry baby cries out for milk (1 Peter 2:2). Timothy's biblical intake was absolutely critical if he was going to "be diligent to present [himself] approved to God as a workman who does not need to be ashamed, accurately handling the word of truth" (2 Tim. 2:15). At the same time, Paul charged him to "avoid worldly and empty chatter, for it will lead to further ungodliness, and their talk will spread like gangrene. Among them are Hymenaeus and Philetus, men who have gone astray from the truth saying that the resurrection has already taken place, and they upset the faith of some" (vv. 16–18).

Pastors are mandated to heed Paul's warning. In spite of that clear command, many expose their biblical illiteracy every time they step into the pulpit. Others are more interested in their own insights and opinions than accurately and fully proclaiming what God has revealed in Scripture. The result is always a weak, shallow congregation that proliferates untrained and unqualified leaders who extend their pastor's ignorance exponentially. Today, the church is overrun with "leaders" who have human skills but no passion for biblical scholarship.

Despite what current trends would have us believe, a godly pastor can be ignorant about pop culture and the latest internet memes. He can be ignorant about psychology and sociology.

He doesn't need to be an expert on world events, social movements, or leadership strategies. Being well versed in movies, music, and sports isn't part of the job description, either, and it's often a hindrance to the actual work of ministry. Rather, a pastor must be an expert in the Bible.

Hand in hand with the consistent study of God's Word is the ability to avoid the things that most often distract from that study. God's people need to be fed out of the overflow of the pastor's deep study of Scripture—not some scraps he was able to pull together at the last minute. Such weakness in the pulpit leads to weakness throughout the church. Good communication skills may entertain, but they are useless if the pastor is not unleashing God's Word.

Describing the effort required to fulfill the pastoral calling, Richard Baxter said:

> The ministerial work must be carried on diligently and laboriously, as being of such unspeakable consequence to ourselves and others. We are seeking to uphold the world, to save it from the curse of God, to perfect the creation, to attain the ends of Christ's death, to save ourselves and others from damnation, to overcome the devil, and demolish his kingdom, to set up the kingdom of Christ, and to attain and help others to the kingdom of glory. And are these works to be done with a careless mind, or a lazy hand? O see, then, that this work be done with all your might! Study hard, for the well is deep, and our brains are shallow.[2]

The simple focus of the man of God is on one Book, and a pastor must labor to master that Book. Ignorance is not an option—it's tantamount to pastoral malpractice. The shepherd's ability to faithfully feed his flock depends on how well he's feeding himself.

## Faithful to Avoid

Along with their faithful study of Scripture, godly pastors must avoid the influence of unbiblical teaching. Paul says, "But have nothing to do with worldly fables fit only for old women" (1 Tim. 4:7). The Apostle employs a strong Greek word (*paraiteomai*, translated "have nothing to do") to convey the seriousness of this duty—it means to "excuse oneself" or "decline to receive." Paul is instructing Timothy to forcefully reject and put away anything unbiblical because it will hinder and poison his ministry.

The word translated as "fables" is *muthoi*, from which we get the English word *myth*. We don't know specifically what "worldly fables" Paul had in mind—the term could apply to anything that opposed or contradicted the truth of Scripture. And referring to such teaching as "fit only for old women" is Paul's sarcastic way of highlighting the foolishness of such dalliances with false doctrine. In the Roman world, women did not have the same educational opportunities as men, and this epithet—common among philosophers of the day—emphasized the teaching's lack of credibility and sophistication. In first-century parlance, such ideas were well beneath an intelligent, educated man.

Scripture encourages all believers to avoid purveyors of false teaching, and those who look down on the Word of God. Psalm 1:1 says, "How blessed is the man who does not walk in the counsel of the wicked, nor stand in the path of sinners, nor sit in the seat of scoffers!" The pastor, even in his education and training, must not keep company or sit in the classes of those who mock God's truth, as such familiarity dilutes his biblical convictions and exposes him to harmful error. That pattern most often shows itself in the academic world. Confident in their own wisdom and understanding, Christians unwittingly expose themselves to deceivers and become sympathetic to erring colleagues, weakening their grip on the truth so they begin to excuse their false doctrine. This slippery slope has led many to apostasy. Others succumb to the siren song of novelty and innovation, becoming more enamored with what is new rather than with what is *true*.

As a minister of the Word of God and a protector and feeder of the sheep, the minister cannot allow his commitment to the Word of God to be polluted in any way. He must protect himself from divided loyalties and detrimental influences. And he must remember that his spiritual safety and soundness directly affect his sheep.

## Faithful to Lead

In 1 Timothy 4:11, Paul identifies another quality of a faithful minister of the Word: authority. He writes, "Prescribe and teach these things." The pastor does not make casual or optional suggestions to his congregation. He's not there to entertain or tickle ears. He's not called to deliver sentimental emotionalism or motivational speeches. He's called to authoritatively assert the Word of God.

Titus 2:15 says: "These things speak and exhort and reprove with all authority. Let no one disregard you." Pastoral ministry demands boldness. It demands conviction—not in one's own authority, but in that which emanates from God's Word. As Peter writes, "Whoever speaks, is to do so as one who is speaking the utterances of God" (1 Peter 4:11). That said, the godly shepherd doesn't bulldoze over his sheep; he's still meek and gentle. But in that patience and gentleness of transmission, there is an unequivocal submission to the authority of Scripture.

It's worth noting that those who have failed in terms of the previous criteria won't have success here, either. Lazy students of God's Word won't bring its authority to bear on their congregations, and those who don't know what it means certainly won't step into the pulpit with conviction and preach with power. Likewise, those who persist in their openness to unbiblical influences will quickly find their confidence in Scripture's absolute authority diminished and corrupted. Put simply, there is no authority in the preaching of men who don't faithfully explain Scripture.

Ultimately, the godly pastor knows the authority doesn't lie with him. He's not the head over his church—Christ is. His congregation has merely been entrusted to him for a time, and it is his job to bring the authority of God's Word to bear on their lives, trusting the Spirit to work through it to accomplish His will.

## Faithful to Teach

Paul also describes the godly minister as one whose relentless devotion is to maintain a thoroughly biblical ministry. He charges Timothy with these words: "Until I come, give attention to the public reading of Scripture, to exhortation and teaching" (1 Tim. 4:13). Paul's words give three straightforward tasks to those in pastoral ministry: expound the Scripture, explain its meaning, and exhort the people to follow it.

The Apostle expands on his exhortation to Timothy in the next verse: "Do not neglect the spiritual gift within you" (v. 14). There are a variety of concerns, issues, and activities that could easily consume a pastor's time. But Paul saw the calling on his life—and on all ministers of the gospel—with distinct clarity. He would later encourage Timothy to "suffer hardship with me, as a good soldier of Christ Jesus. No soldier in active service entangles himself in the affairs of everyday life, so that he may please the one who enlisted him as a soldier" (2 Tim. 2:3–4). The faithful shepherd keeps his time, his efforts, and his ministry focused on the Word of God.

It's interesting that this is all that is said about a pastor's specific duties. Similarly, when Paul explained the qualifications for elders and leaders earlier in his first epistle to Timothy, the only real function described is "able to teach" (1 Tim. 3:2). There's nothing here about being a dynamic leader, a master strategist, a chairman of the board, a vision caster, or any of the other pastoral models prevalent in churches today. It just says he is to *teach the Word*.

The church is often guilty of having too low a view of pastoral ministry—look at any list of the most popular and influential pastors for all the proof you need. But today, there is also a sense in which too much is made of the pastor's ministry—that it must entail recording podcasts, writing books, earning doctorates, speaking at conferences, and achieving global recognition. That's simply not how the Lord measures the faithfulness or success of a pastor. His standard is much higher. A pastor must faithfully feed the Word to the flock the Lord has given him. The New Testament knows nothing of a pastor without a flock—a local church.

## Stay Faithful

Finally, Paul tells us that an excellent shepherd perseveres in his work. His words to Timothy are direct: "Pay close attention to yourself and to your teaching; persevere in these things, for as you do this you will ensure salvation both for yourself and for those who hear you" (1 Tim. 4:16). The word "persevere" is *epimenō* in the Greek—it's an intense way of saying "to stay" or "to remain." As much as he can, a pastor should work to see an enduring ministry of faithfully exposing the Word of God and living out what he preaches.

Consistency is rare in the church today. Evangelicalism is dominated by personalities who write books and speak at conferences without the accountability of a regular pulpit ministry or a local congregation to serve. That should not be the goal for a pastor—to outgrow his church and graduate to the conference or media circuit. Faithful shepherds aren't looking to get away from their sheep.

Believers must fight the instinct to become enamored of such celebrities—it's unhealthy for them and for their pastors. The Lord has put His shepherds where He wants them. And to those shepherds, Paul simply says, in effect, "Go, and plan to stay."

What's remarkable is how the other qualities flourish in an enduring ministry of godliness and biblical teaching. The church matures in its ability to spot spiritual error and defend the truth of Scripture. The people learn to study the Bible for themselves, deepening their affection for the Lord. They lose the taste for worldliness, trivialities, and anything that takes their attention away from the truth. They cultivate a reverence for God's Word, willingly submitting to its authority over their lives. And they develop a taste for biblical teaching and godly teachers who exalt and explain the Word of God.

May the Lord raise up a generation of faithful shepherds to feed and protect His flock.

## Chapter Six

# THE BIBLE IS
# FOOD FOR THE SOUL

Some Christians undergo a frantic struggle every Sunday to remember where they last saw their Bibles. They know they had it with them at church last week. But they haven't seen it since they got home and set it down. Inevitably, they'll find it buried somewhere under the debris of the intervening week. And once the next Sunday rolls around, they will launch the same search to locate it again in time for its once-a-week use.

Describing the dangerous distance that sometimes exists between believers and their Bibles, Charles Spurgeon said:

> Most people treat the Bible very politely. They have a small pocket volume, neatly bound; they put a white pocket-handkerchief around it, and carry it to their places of worship; when they get home, they lay it up in a drawer till next Sunday morning; then it comes out again for a little bit of a treat and goes to chapel; that

is all the poor Bible gets in the way of an airing. That is your style of entertaining this heavenly messenger. There is dust enough on some of your Bibles to write "damnation" with your fingers.[1]

Spurgeon noted that trend more than 150 years ago. Today, in a culture that excels at distraction, shallow thought, and casual indifference, it's even easier to neglect one's Bible. Some don't even bother to keep a physical copy of God's Word; instead it's just another app on their phones or words projected on a screen. Christians cannot afford to have such a dismissive, lackadaisical approach to Scripture. As the only repository of God's written revelation to us, Scripture demands our attention.

It sounds incongruous that believers would need to be reminded to faithfully study and hold fast to the Word. But in his first epistle, Peter exhorts his readers about the way God's people ought to hunger for His truth:

Therefore, putting aside all malice and all deceit and hypocrisy and envy and all slander, like newborn babies, long for the pure milk of the word, so that by it you may grow in respect to salvation, if you have tasted the kindness of the Lord. And coming to Him as to a living stone which has been rejected by men, but is choice and precious in the sight of God, you also, as living stones, are being built up as a spiritual house for a holy priesthood, to offer up spiritual sacrifices acceptable to God through Jesus Christ. (1 Peter 2:1–5)

Peter gives us a lot to unpack in that passage, but at its core is the imperative to "long for the pure milk of the word." This is not a suggestion. It's an unequivocal directive—one reinforced by everything else in the surrounding context. Peter's primary emphasis here is the command to cultivate an abiding desire for Scripture.

A hunger for the truth is one of the defining characteristics of those who have been redeemed by God. Jesus indicated as much: "He who is of God hears the words of God" (John 8:47). Paul expressed a similar love for God's Word in the believer's heart: "I joyfully concur with the law of God in the inner man" (Rom. 7:22). Job said, "I have treasured the words of His mouth more than my necessary food" (Job 23:12). Psalm 1 says that the godly man is blessed because "his delight is in the law of the Lord, and in His law he meditates day and night" (v. 2). In Psalm 19, David describes his own affection for God's truth, saying it is "more desirable than gold, yes, than much fine gold; sweeter also than honey and the drippings of the honeycomb" (v. 10). And in Psalm 40:8, he writes, "I delight to do Your will, O my God; Your Law is within my heart."

But the magnum opus regarding love for God's Word is undoubtedly Psalm 119. Over and over, the psalmist recounts the glories of Scripture, extolling its perfections and expressing the satisfaction found only therein. He rejoices in the truth, not from external compulsion, but from the overflow of his heart. He has seen firsthand the outworking of God's Word in his life, and he can't hold back his grateful adoration for all that it has already accomplished, and all that it will in the future.

In verse 174, the psalmist's praise for the truth culminates with the statement, "I long for Your salvation, O LORD, and Your law is my delight." The Word is his strongest desire and greatest delight. Psalm 42:1 communicates a similar longing: "As the deer pants for the water brooks, so my soul pants for You, O God." In the Septuagint, both those verses are translated with the same Greek verb (*epipotheō*) Peter uses to describe how believers must "long for the pure milk of the word." The term communicates an intense, compelling craving. In James 4:5, it is translated as "jealously desires." Paul used the same word to describe his desire for heaven (2 Cor. 5:2). Throughout Scripture, it is employed to reflect an intense, recurring passion and an insatiable longing.

## The Urgency of Infancy

Peter demands that his readers cultivate that kind of hunger for the Word. And he chooses a powerful analogy to illustrate his point. He says, "Like newborn babies, long for the pure milk of the word" (1 Peter 2:2). He reaches into the physical world to find the most apt and vivid illustration he can employ.

Babies crave milk, and *only* milk. Parents care about the color of the blanket, the pattern of curtains, the decorations in and around the crib, and the way the child is dressed. The baby doesn't care about any of that. Babies don't scream because they're offended by the color of their pajamas. They scream because they want milk. The only thing that matters to them is milk—from the moment they're born, that's their only priority.

It's amazing that everything about a baby is so wonderfully soft and cuddly and inviting—except for their voices. A baby's scream can be piercing and horrific. It's almost completely alien to everything else about the baby; such an awful sound shouldn't come out of that adorable mouth. But it's necessarily so—those irritating screams are designed to ensure that we don't forget to feed the baby. The child will scream his head off to make sure we know it is time to eat. Moreover, babies don't care about the convenience of their needs or how they fit into the rest of our plans. There are no negotiations to engage in—until his needs are met, that baby is going to let us hear it. And it is that singular focus Peter wants to draw our minds to regarding our own hunger for the Word.

Do we have that kind of singular craving for the truth of Scripture? Do we get to the place, like Job, where we desire God's Word more than our necessary food? It would be hard for most people to think of *anything* they desired that strongly—especially in our culture of instant gratification. Virtually everything we truly need or want is never more than a few dollars, a short drive, or a couple mouse clicks away. The kind of helpless hunger Peter describes isn't satisfied so quickly.

And while Peter is commanding us to have that kind of longing for the Word, the longing itself is not the product of external forces or legalistic fears. Nor should our hunger for the truth be a function of begrudging religious duty. It is to rise out of our hearts because of the profound need for it, the way the cries of hunger rise out of a baby's need. There should be such a compelling discontent that we cry out for divine truth as the food for our souls.

That's a far cry from the conversations some Christians have from week to week as they try to locate their Bibles in time for church, or debate whether they should bother going at all. Such attitudes deprive believers of their spiritual sustenance and stifle their usefulness to the kingdom of God.

Sanctification doesn't happen by osmosis. We can't starve ourselves spiritually and still expect to grow in the likeness of Christ. All the facets of Scripture we've discussed—all its rich benefits and blessings—are not available to those who fail or refuse to open it and study.

Others do want to see the Word at work in their lives. They simply need someone to point them in the right direction, to show them how to cultivate such a longing for and ability to understand the truth, and to spur them on to pursue the riches found only in God's Word. For believers like that, Peter offers good help. Under the inspiration of the Holy Spirit, he lays out the critical components for developing a deep hunger and desire for the Word of God.

## Remembering Our Life Source

The initial step in developing our hunger for God's Word is to remember our life source. First Peter 2:1 begins with the word "Therefore," linking the Apostle's exhortation to his prior statements, specifically, verses 23–25 of chapter 1, where he writes: "You have been born again not of seed which is perishable but imperishable, that is, through the living and enduring word of God. For, 'All flesh is like grass, and all its glory like the flower of grass. The grass withers, and the flower falls off, but the word of the Lord endures forever.' And this is the word which was preached to you." Peter wants us to understand that it was the incorruptible, imperishable Word of God that has saved us and transformed us into new creations.

To grasp the full weight of what Peter is saying, we need to remember the spiritual situation we languished in prior to our regeneration. We possessed an unrepentant heart that was "more deceitful than all else and [was] desperately sick; who can understand it?" (Jer. 17:9). In Romans 3, Paul uses quotes from the Old Testament to describe the comprehensive nature of our former depravity: "There is none righteous, not even one; there is none who understands, there is none who seeks for God; all have turned aside, together they have become useless; there is none who does good, there is not even one" (vv. 10–12). He sums up the corruption of that rebellious state thus: "There is no fear of God before their eyes" (v. 18). Not only were we incapable of escaping our depravity, but we were also unwilling to do so. Before the Spirit did His illuminating work through the Word, we had no fear of the Lord or the due penalty of our sins.

Out of that horrendous state, Peter says we "have been born again not of seed which is perishable but imperishable, that is, through the living and enduring word of God" (1 Peter 1:23). Peter identifies this living, enduring Word of God as the source of our spiritual transformation. Borrowing a metaphor from the life and ministry of Christ, Peter describes the Word as an imperishable seed. Just as Jesus explained to His disciples in Matthew 13, a faithful sower cast seed onto soil prepared by the Spirit, and the seed bore fruit. Describing the Bible's transforming power, James says, "In the exercise of His will He brought us forth by the word of truth, so that we would be a kind of first fruits among His creatures" (James 1:18). Referring to the saving work of the Word, John writes in his gospel, "These have been written so that you may believe that Jesus is the Christ, the Son of God; and that believing you may have life in His name" (John 20:31). And in response to all that Scripture has already accomplished in our lives, Peter charges us to cultivate a hunger for it.

Why? Because the power of God's Word does not fade, diminish, or wither (1 Peter 1:24). It is both the source of our transformation *and* the source of our sanctification. It constitutes our spiritual sustenance (Matt. 4:4). It gives us stability and security: "Therefore everyone who hears these words of Mine and acts on them, may be compared to a wise man who built his house on the rock" (Matt. 7:24). Scripture is "the word of [God's] grace, which is able to build you up and to give you the inheritance among all those who are sanctified" (Acts 20:32). It is "the word of life" (Phil. 2:16). Regarding its power, the writer of Hebrews says, "The word of God is living and active and sharper than any two-edged sword, and piercing as far as the division of soul and spirit, of both joints and marrow, and able to judge the thoughts and intentions of the heart" (Heb. 4:12). It is the living Word of God, active and powerful for the salvation, sustenance, and sanctification of His people.

Believers recognize the Word for what it is and for what it does in their lives. Writing to the Thessalonians, Paul said, "For this reason we also constantly thank God that when you received the word of God which you heard from us, you accepted it not as the word of men, but for what it really is, the word of God, which also performs its work in you who believe" (1 Thess. 2:13). Scripture was instrumental in our salvation, and it continues to perform God's work in us. Moreover, we know it accomplishes God's work without fail. "For as the rain and the snow come down from heaven, and do not return there without watering the earth and making it bear and sprout, and furnishing seed to the sower and bread to the eater; so will My word be which goes forth from My mouth; it will not return to Me empty, without accomplishing what I desire, and without succeeding in the matter for which I sent it" (Isa. 55:10–11).

If we want to experience the supernatural work of God in our lives, we must understand that the Holy Spirit makes it happen only through His Word. There is no other means He has ordained, no momentary emotional or existential experience that can catapult us to some higher level of spiritual maturity. We cannot set aside our Bibles and expect His sanctifying work to continue uninterrupted. God saved us through the power of His Word, and its work is not finished. We need to increase our hunger for His truth, knowing that it is the sole source of our spiritual lives and the only means through which the Spirit conforms us into the image of His Son.

## Eliminating Our Sin

Peter highlights a second component in desiring the Word—we must also eliminate our sin. He writes, "Therefore, putting aside all malice and all deceit and hypocrisy and envy and all slander" (1 Peter 2:1). He says we must take a look at our lives and start shedding sinful thoughts and activities. The Greek verb he uses here (*apothemenoi*) refers to stripping off soiled garments. It conveys the same idea Paul had in mind when he wrote: "But now you also, put them all aside: anger, wrath, malice, slander, and abusive speech from your mouth. Do not lie to one another, since you laid aside the old self with its evil practices" (Col. 3:8–9). In the early church, believers would be baptized in their old clothes, and when they came out of the waters they would be given new clothes to put on. The process was symbolic of the fact that salvation marked the shedding of all that was old and the putting on of all that was new. Peter depicts a similar idea in the language he uses here.

Having begun our new lives in Christ, we must shed and set aside whatever is still hanging on from our residual fallenness. We need to identify these lingering elements of the old life as direct hindrances to our desire for God's Word. They spoil our spiritual appetites, as the stench of the old contaminates the fragrance of the new.

To help with the shedding process, Peter identifies several sinful categories that might still be lingering in our lives. The first he mentions is "all malice." This isn't malice in the narrow sense we usually think of; it's not merely evil intentions directed toward another person. The word here (*kakia*) serves as an all-inclusive term for wickedness. It encompasses everything base, disgraceful, and wretched. It is the general, pervasive malignancy of the flesh, out of which evil behaviors emerge. Peter is referring to the generic, inherited wickedness common to all people. First and foremost, that is what believers must eliminate if we are going to have a proper desire for the Word.

To that, Peter adds "all deceit." The Greek word *dolos* was used to describe the bait on a fishhook. Here it refers to all forms of deception, dishonesty, guile, treachery, and falsehood. Whereas wickedness speaks to general, open sin, deceit is by nature more discreet. Peter is describing the secret, hidden ways we sin against and take advantage of others. Believers must not traffic in such deceptions. Duplicity is incompatible with a hunger for God's truth.

Continuing on the theme of secret sin, Peter also charges believers to put off "hypocrisy." This refers to any pretense or insincerity, anything phony or inconsistent. Believers must be genuine in all they say and do. God's Word has no tolerance for those who practice hypocrisy.

Peter points to another sin believers must eliminate: "envy." Believers must not resent the prosperity of others or covet their possessions. This category also includes the hatred, bitterness, grudges, and conflicts that corrupt relationships in this ruined world. Peter is talking about the kinds of interpersonal sins that inhibit our usefulness to the kingdom and stifle our appetite for God's Word.

Finally, Peter commands his readers to put aside "all slander." He uses an onomatopoeic word (*katalalias*) to describe slanderous whispers and tattling behind another's back. It also includes defamation, disparagement, malicious gossip, or any other attempt to tear down others.

There is a natural progression to the sins Peter describes. He starts with the broad sense of general wickedness and corruption that produces deceit and deception. Deceit leads to hypocrisy, while hypocrisy, in turn, masks envy. And festering envy will inevitably lead to slander.

Peter wants the opposite for God's people. In the previous chapter, he urges his readers to "fervently love one another from the heart" (1 Peter 1:22). In order to do that, Christians have to weed out the wickedness that lingers from their former, sinful selves. They need to look inside at the nature of their hearts, uncovering the secret sins of deceit and hypocrisy. And they must bring an end to the sins that poison and corrupt their relationships with others, like envy and slander. Peter wants believers to identify and eliminate all the filthy rags of the flesh. God's people need to faithfully confess and repent of the sin that remains in their lives, pleading with Him to remove it.

We understand that true repentance is the work of the Holy Spirit. But the Spirit does not perform that work in the lives of unwilling people; we have to cry out for Him to bring about repentance in us. And an essential element of that cleansing, refining work is the Word of God (John 15:3). We need to cultivate a desire for Scripture and the work it accomplishes in us. We need to hunger to learn its truths, to receive its joys and its convicting realities. We need to eagerly and attentively sit under its teaching and study it for ourselves as though our spiritual lives depend on it—because they do.

If you don't have that kind of hunger for the cleansing, refining work of the Word, you need to carefully examine your life to see if there is sin hindering your desire.

## Admitting Our Need

The third step in rekindling our desire for God's Word is to admit our need. Peter charges us, "Like newborn babies, long for the pure milk of the word" (1 Peter 2:2). There is no mistaking Peter's intention here; the term *artigennēta brephē* refers to a suckling infant in the first moments after his birth. This isn't just any nursing baby—Peter is reaching all the way back to the initial moments after a child emerges from his mother's womb, and the immediacy and intensity of his hunger. In the instant that baby is born, he goes right to his mother to provide the pure, uncontaminated milk he desperately needs. That milk is vital to the baby's survival, as it provides both nourishment and antibodies to protect and sustain that little life.

It's important that we don't confuse the point of Peter's metaphor with others in Scripture. He is not merely talking about newborn babies in Christ—this isn't limited to new believers. All Christians, regardless of their spiritual maturity, need to cultivate a singular craving for God's truth. Likewise, Peter is not talking about the milk of the Word versus the meat (cf. 1 Cor. 3:2; Heb. 5:12–14). That's a separate metaphor used by other authors to illustrate a different point. Here,

Peter is simply exhorting his readers to hunger for the whole Word of God.

We ought to be thankful for such a clear, graphic analogy. A newborn baby longs for his mother's milk because he cannot survive without it. And in God's design, various mechanisms go off in that precious little baby to create agitation and irritation when his primary need is not met. This is not just a mild hunger—it's a critical, all-consuming need that touches every area of life.

This is a hunger that should be apparent in the life of every believer. However, many Christians have instead cultivated an appetite for spiritual junk food. They prefer shallow sermons, feel-good stories, worldly entertainment, emotional experiences, and sensory overload to clear, verse-by-verse Bible teaching. Many in the church have cut themselves off from the source of true spiritual food, choosing instead to perpetually languish in an unhealthy, underdeveloped state.

Others are simply starving. My heart goes out to those true believers who can't find a reliable church that provides real spiritual food. I hear from people in that situation all the time. They're committed to their local church, but they're not being faithfully fed. They have to survive with weak teaching, scrounging for morsels instead of feasting on the riches of God's Word. And in that malnourished state, they develop deficient immune systems, succumbing to heresies and errors they would otherwise know to avoid. That's the cost of weak preaching and weak pastors—they leave the people under them exposed and vulnerable to lies that would not confuse or corrupt stronger believers. Today, too many pulpits are occupied by hirelings who don't know the first thing about how to feed their flocks—they're either incapable of feeding God's sheep or unwilling to do so. My prayer is that believers caught in such situations would find faithful ministries to help supplement the spiritual sustenance they require from God's Word.

Ultimately, Peter wants his readers to understand their dependence on the truth and develop a proper hunger for it in light of that consuming need. There is no alternate supply of spiritual nourishment. We don't have the luxury of options—there is no buffet table or smorgasbord to pick and choose from. In a world full of corrupting influences and contaminating ideas, there is only one source of the pure spiritual milk we require: Scripture. And we should hunger for it accordingly.

## Pursuing Our Growth

The second half of 1 Peter 2:2 highlights a fourth step in developing a hunger for biblical truth. Explaining why God's people ought to hunger for the pure milk of His Word, Peter writes, "so that by it you may grow in respect to salvation."

No true believer is completely satisfied with his spiritual progress. Under the illuminating, sanctifying influence of the Holy Spirit, all of us are aware of areas in our lives that still need to be refined and disciplined for the sake of godliness. In fact, the more we mature, the more capable we are of spotting the sin that still remains in our hearts. The Apostle Paul is a prime example. In many ways, he is the model for believers.

But in his first epistle to Timothy, he refers to himself as the chief of sinners (1 Tim. 1:15). In anguish over the sinful flesh he cannot escape or overcome, he cried out: "Wretched man that I am! Who will set me free from the body of this death?" (Rom. 7:24). Paul understood the weakness that remained in him, and he longed to be set free from the frailties and failings of his flesh. To that end, the singular goal of his life was Christ-likeness and spiritual growth. In his letter to the Philippian church, he describes his earnest pursuit:

> But whatever things were gain to me, those things I have counted as loss for the sake of Christ. More than that, I count all things to be loss in view of the surpassing value of knowing Christ Jesus my Lord, for whom I have suffered the loss of all things, and count them but rubbish so that I may gain Christ, and may be found in Him, not having a righteousness of my own derived from the Law, but that which is through faith in Christ, the righteousness which comes from God on the basis of faith, that I may know Him and the power of His resurrection and the fellowship of His sufferings, being conformed to His death; in order that I may attain to the resurrection from the dead. Not that I have already obtained it or have already become perfect, but I press on so that I may lay hold of that for which also I was laid hold of by Christ Jesus. Brethren, I do not regard myself as having laid hold of it yet; but one thing I do: forgetting what lies behind and reaching forward to what lies ahead, I

press on toward the goal for the prize of the upward call of God in Christ Jesus. (Phil. 3:7–14)

Paul carried a similar burden of spiritual discontent for those under his care. He referred to the Galatians as "my children, with whom I am again in labor until Christ is formed in you" (Gal. 4:19). Part of the godly shepherd's duty is to help those in the church see their remaining sin and their need for further sanctification. He needs to help them develop a discontentment with their spiritual state and to spur them on to greater growth and godliness. It's not the pastor's job to affirm our lifestyles, dangle false promises of health and wealth, or validate our personal ambitions for life. He's not there to make us feel good about ourselves or convince us that God loves us just the way we are and wants to give us whatever we want. On the contrary, he's there to hammer on our hearts, burdening them just as his own heart is burdened, with the understanding that we fall far short of what we should be in Christ. All of us— pastors, elders, and laypeople alike—must constantly go back to the Word to understand the high standard of God's righteousness and to be reminded of just how often we fail to live up to it. We need to examine ourselves regularly through the lens of Scripture, developing a spiritual discontentment that motivates us to faithfully pursue greater sanctification. There is discontentment in the cry of a newborn baby who can't do anything to fulfill his own needs. There needs to be a similar discontentment in us—one that draws us back to Scripture as the only source of our spiritual sustenance and growth.

Rather than sitting self-satisfied and stagnant, Peter says believers need to "grow in respect to salvation" (1 Peter 2:2). God's people need to grow, and they can only do so through the ministry of His Spirit through His Word. In the words of Paul, we need to be "transformed into the [Lord's] image from glory to glory" (2 Cor. 3:18). And how do we mark that progress? How do we know we're advancing in our spiritual growth?

We can point to several factors that mark our spiritual growth. The first is an increase in spiritual understanding. True sanctification goes hand in hand with a deeper, richer understanding of the Bible. It doesn't happen in some kind of spiritual fog or through mystical experience. Too many people in the church today claim to have received spiritual insight through their dreams, their gut feelings, or hearing God's voice in their heads. That is not the means to true spiritual growth—if anything, it's leading them away from the truth and further into darkness. We don't need to look inside ourselves for truth or wait to receive personal insight from the Lord. True spiritual growth starts with an increase in our spiritual understanding, which requires an increase in our biblical knowledge. As our theology deepens, as our grasp of Scripture strengthens, that fuels our spiritual growth.

Along with an increase in spiritual understanding comes joy—a deeper delight in the things of God. We don't hold our theology with cold, remote resolve—we develop a warm, rich affection for the God of Scripture. We enthusiastically praise the Lord for who He is and what He has done. We celebrate the work of His Word in our lives, and we long to see it unleashed in the lives of those around us.

One of the reasons I love to speak at pastors' conferences is the opportunity for corporate worship. In those rooms packed with preachers and church leaders, the worship is not tentative or passive. Just the opposite—the walls reverberate with loud voices belting out their love for the Lord, His gospel, and His church. They're singing their convictions, proclaiming in song the truths of Scripture that have captured their hearts and minds. Their delight is in the Word, and the same should be true of everyone who is growing spiritually.

A third factor that marks the progress of sanctification is a greater love for God. If we're growing in our understanding of Scripture, then we're growing in our appreciation for the majesty of our Lord. We're more intimately acquainted with His person and work. We're more enamored of His goodness, His mercy, and the rich blessings He pours out on us every day. The deeper our understanding of Scripture goes, the more deeply we get to know God in the fullness of His revelation to us.

Think of it this way: if you're not growing in your love for God, there is good reason to believe that you are treating Scripture superficially.

Another vital component of spiritual growth is strengthened faith. With an increased knowledge of Scripture and a greater love for God, we become able to trust Him through all of life's trials. I've spoken to many believers who have just received news of a terminal disease or another dire diagnosis. Often, their primary prayer request isn't for healing, but that God would use them as a witness for Himself in the time they have left. There's no collapsing in the face of trials, no despair in the midst of the storm. Their faith is firmly rooted in the goodness of God and His glorious purposes for their lives. If we're growing spiritually, we're more steadfast in our faith and surer of God's sovereign care and provision. In a restless world, we can rest in His goodness.

The believer's spiritual growth is also measured by his constant obedience. As the Apostle John succinctly says: "By this we know that we have come to know Him, if we keep His commandments. The one who says, 'I have come to know Him,' and does not keep His commandments, is a liar, and the truth is not in him; but whoever keeps His word, in him the love of God has truly been perfected. By this we know that we are in Him: the one who says he abides in Him ought himself to walk in the same manner as He walked" (1 John 2:3–6). Spiritual growth is the process of growing in Christlikeness—how we think, talk, and act must always be conforming to the Lord's righteous standard.

If we're being sanctified by the Spirit through the Scriptures, it will be evident through an increase in our spiritual understanding, a deeper delight in the things of the Lord, a greater love for God, a strengthening faith in Him, and a consistent pattern of obedience to His Word. That is the kind of spiritual growth Peter wants us to pursue.

## Surveying Our Blessings

Finally, Peter gives his readers a fifth step in developing a hunger for God's Word. After we have remembered our life source, eliminated our sin, admitted our need, and pursued our growth, there is one final component: surveying our blessings. There is a hint of sarcasm in his words: "if you have tasted the kindness of the Lord." (1 Peter 2:3). Of course, the believers he was writing to had tasted the kindness of the Lord—they were well acquainted with His goodness and grace through their conversion and through the daily blessings He poured out in their lives.

We as believers ought to make a habit of recounting the goodness, kindness, and mercy of the Lord in our lives. We ought to remember, as Paul enthusiastically writes, that "God, being rich in mercy, because of His great love with which He loved us, even when we were dead in our transgressions, made us alive together with Christ (by grace you have been saved), and raised us up with Him, and seated us with Him in the heavenly places in Christ Jesus, so that in the ages to come He might show the surpassing riches of His grace in kindness toward us in Christ Jesus" (Eph. 2:4–7). We ought to rejoice that "when the kindness of God our Savior and His love for mankind appeared, He saved us, not on the basis of deeds which we have done in righteousness, but according to His mercy, by the washing of regeneration and renewing by the Holy Spirit" (Titus 3:4–5). We who belong to Christ have, in the words of the psalmist, "[tasted] and [seen] that the LORD is good" (Ps. 34:8). He "has blessed us with every spiritual blessing in the heavenly places in Christ" (Eph. 1:3). We know firsthand that "the LORD's lovingkindnesses indeed never cease, for His compassions never fail. They are new every morning; great is Your faithfulness" (Lam. 3:22–23).

Regardless of temporal trials and hardships, Scripture is clear that believers live blessed lives in the kindness and abundant provision of God. The Bible is replete with examples of His loving-kindness, patience, mercy, grace, and faithfulness to undeserving sinners. We should not grow tired of reading the account of His consistent goodness throughout His Word. Nor should we neglect to praise Him for the lavish blessings He faithfully provides to us.

In case his readers struggled to recall God's faithfulness and goodness to them, Peter goes on to recount many of the spiritual privileges granted to those who know and love the Lord:

And coming to Him as to a living stone which has been rejected by men, but is choice and precious in the sight of God, you also, as living stones, are being built up as a spiritual house for a holy priesthood, to offer up spiritual sacrifices acceptable to God through Jesus Christ. For this is contained in Scripture: "Behold, I lay in Zion a choice stone, a precious corner stone, and he who believes in Him will not be disappointed." This precious value, then, is for you who believe; but for those who disbelieve, "The stone which the builders rejected, this became the very corner stone," and, "A stone of stumbling and a rock of offense"; for they stumble because they are disobedient to the word, and to this doom they were also appointed. But you are a chosen race, a royal priesthood, a holy nation, a people for God's own possession, so that you may proclaim the excellencies of Him who has called you out of darkness into His marvelous light; for you once were not a people, but now you are the people of God; you had not received mercy, but now you have received mercy. (1 Peter 2:4–10)

We can't fully unpack the riches of this passage in the space remaining, but we can briefly glimpse the spiritual privileges Peter wants us to cherish. He begins with the phrase, "And coming to Him" (v. 4). We have *access to God*. That alone sets the Christian faith apart from false religions, including the dominant religions of the first-century world. We do not require an intermediary—we don't have to go through a priest, a mystic, or the saints of old. We don't have to petition Mary to get the Lord's attention. Through the indwelling Holy Spirit, we have instant, uninterrupted access to the Creator and Sustainer of the universe. We live in His constant presence.

Moreover, we enjoy this constant communion with "a living stone" (v. 4), and not merely a carved rock or some other dead idol. Put simply, our God is not stone dead—*He lives*. He has an active presence in our lives, convicting us of sin, growing us in His likeness, and using us as He sovereignly orchestrates the work of His kingdom.

Verse 5 continues, "You also, as living stones, are being built up as a spiritual house." To be living stones is to be united with Christ, our cornerstone. This is the glorious reality of the relationship Paul described in his letter to the Ephesians: "So then you are no longer strangers and aliens, but you are fellow citizens with the saints, and are of God's household, having been built on the foundation of the apostles and prophets, Christ Jesus Himself being the corner stone, in whom the whole building, being fitted together, is growing into a holy temple in the Lord, in whom you also are being built together into a dwelling of God in the Spirit" (Eph. 2:19–22). Believers have the privilege of unity with Christ in the ongoing work of God as He continues to build His church.

Within the "spiritual house" God is constructing, He has set us aside as "a holy priesthood" (1 Peter 2:5). Consider this: believers have greater immediate access to God than any of Israel's priests ever enjoyed. Only the high priest could enter the presence of God in the Holy of Holies, and even then only once a year. Instead, we can "draw near with confidence to the throne of grace, so that we may receive mercy and find grace to help in time of need" (Heb. 4:16). Later, the writer of Hebrews explains why we can draw near to God: "We have confidence to enter the holy place by the blood of Jesus" (Heb. 10:19). Israel's sacrificial system was insufficient to save—it pointed ahead to Christ and to the redemption He alone could provide. Only on this side of the cross can we confidently and constantly approach God, because our assurance is not in ourselves but in the completed work of His Son.

As God's holy priesthood, we have been called "to offer up spiritual sacrifices" (1 Peter 2:5). What is a spiritual sacrifice? Paul describes it for us in his epistle to the Romans: "Therefore I urge you, brethren, by the mercies of God, to present your bodies a living and holy sacrifice, acceptable to God, which is your spiritual service of worship. And do not be conformed to this world, but be transformed by the renewing of your mind, so that you may prove what the will of God is, that which is good and acceptable and perfect" (Rom. 12:1–2). We are spiritual sacrifices—our minds, bodies, deeds, words, and everything else about us ought to be sacrificed to the praise and glory of God. We're not concerned with expressing our individuality or parading our "authenticity" (tragically, that has become a byword in the church for flaunting one's sin). Rather, we sacrifice our lives and wills, striving to obey and serve the Lord out of our desire to be conformed to His image. As His holy priesthood, we could give nothing better than this—and it's a privilege to give ourselves up for the sake of His kingdom.

In 1 Peter 2:6–8, Peter continues to identify the believer's abundant privileges. We have *security* in Christ: "For this is contained in Scripture: 'Behold, I lay in Zion a choice stone, a precious corner stone, and he who believes in Him will not be disappointed'" (v. 6). Unlike the unbelieving world, we have *affection* for Christ: "This precious value, then, is for you who believe; but for those who disbelieve, 'The stone which the builders rejected, this became the very corner stone,' and, 'A stone of stumbling and a rock of offense'; for they stumble because they are disobedient to the word, and to this doom they were also appointed" (vv. 7–8).

Peter uses several short phrases to highlight more of our privileges in verse 9: "But you are a chosen race, a royal priesthood, a holy nation, a people for God's own possession, so that you may proclaim the excellencies of Him who has called you out of darkness into His marvelous light." Following the Apostle's inspired train of thought, we have been blessed through God's work of *election*, setting us apart for salvation before the foundations of the world (cf. Eph. 1:4–5). We look forward to our future *dominion* with Christ in His kingdom (cf. Rev. 5:10; 20:6). We've been called out and *separated* from the corruption of this world (cf. Rom. 6:4–6; 2 Cor. 5:17). We've been bought through the sacrifice of Christ, and we are now the permanent *possessions* of God (cf. John 10:28–29; 1 Peter 1:18–19). In saving and separating us, God has set us to the task of *proclaiming* His glorious gospel (cf. Matt. 28:19–20; Col. 3:16–17). And we know firsthand the power of His gospel, as it has *illuminated* and transformed us (cf. Ps. 119:105; Col. 1:13).

Finally, the passage concludes with one last privilege in 1 Peter 2:10: "For you once were not a people, but now you are the people of God; you had not received mercy, but now you have received mercy." Here Peter draws our attention to the blessing of God's *compassion*. This isn't merely the compassion of God's common grace and the mercy He daily shows to all. This is the compassion that God's people have experienced through His saving, regenerating, and sanctifying work.

Human language is insufficient to describe that aspect of God's compassion in its fullness. The psalmist attempts to describe its scope, writing, "For as high as the heavens are above the earth, so great is His lovingkindness toward those who fear Him" (Ps. 103:11). In Psalm 65:4, David cries out in praise of God's compassion, "How blessed is the one whom You choose and bring near to You to dwell in Your courts." Paul likewise reflects on the blessings poured out on us through God's compassionate, saving work: "And we know that God causes all things to work together for good to those who love God, to those who are called according to His purpose. For those whom He foreknew, He also predestined to become conformed to the image of His Son, so that He would be the firstborn among many brethren; and these whom He predestined, He also called; and these whom He called, He also justified; and these whom He justified, He also glorified" (Rom. 8:28–30). In His immense compassion, the Lord has redeemed us from the penalty of our sins, transformed us into His likeness, and secured us for an eternity with Him.

Altogether, these are the rich, indescribable privileges we enjoy in Christ—the abundant spiritual blessings that should prompt us to cultivate a consistent hunger for God's Word.

# NOTES

## Chapter 1

1 Elizabeth Rundle Charles, *Chronicles of the Schönberg-Cotta Family* (London: T. Nelson and Sons, 1864), 276.

2 Jack Rogers and Donald McKim, *The Authority and Interpretation of the Bible* (San Francisco: Harper and Row, 1979), xxii.

3 "The Jesus Seminar," Westar Institute, accessed August 31, 2018, https://www.westarinstitute.org/projects/the-jesus-seminar.

4 John Dart, "Seminar Rules Out 80% of Words Attributed to Jesus," March 4, 1991, *Los Angeles Times*, http://articles.latimes.com/1991-03-04/news/mn-77_1_jesus-seminar.

5 Robert Brow, "Evangelical Megashift," *Christianity Today*, February 19, 1990, http://www.brow.on.ca/Articles/Megashift.html.

6 Brow, "Evangelical Megashift."

7 Brow, "Evangelical Megashift."

## Chapter 2

1 J.P. Moreland, *Love Your God with All Your Mind* (Colorado Springs, Colo.: NavPress, 1997), 21.

2 Moreland, *Love Your God*, 21.

3 Charles Haddon Spurgeon, "Thus Saith the Lord," sermon 591 in *The Metropolitan Tabernacle Pulpit*, vol. 10 (London: Passmore and Alabaster, 1864), 535–36.

4 Andy Stanley, "Aftermath, Part 3: Not Difficult," sermon delivered April 30, 2018, at North Point Community Church, Alpharetta, Ga.

5 Andy Stanley, *Deep and Wide* (Grand Rapids, Mich.: Zondervan, 2012), 246.

## Chapter 4

1 John Bunyan, *The Whole Works of John Bunyan* (London: Blackie and Son, 1862), 2:594.

## Chapter 5

1 For a detailed exposition of 1 Timothy 4:6–16, see *The MacArthur New Testament Commentary: 1 Timothy*, chapters 14 and 15.

2 Richard Baxter, *The Reformed Pastor* (Edinburgh, Scotland: Banner of Truth, 1979), 112.

## Chapter 6

1 Charles Haddon Spurgeon, "The Bible," sermon 15 in *The New Park Street Pulpit*, vol. 1 (London: Passmore & Alabaster, 1855), 112.

# SCRIPTURE INDEX

# ABOUT THE AUTHOR

Dr. John MacArthur is pastor-teacher of Grace Community Church in Sun Valley, Calif., president of The Master's University and Seminary, and president and featured teacher with the Grace to You media ministry.

Founded in 1969, Grace to You is the nonprofit organization responsible for developing, producing, and distributing Dr. MacArthur's books, audio resources, and the *Grace to You* radio and television programs. *Grace to You* radio airs more than fifteen hundred times daily throughout the English-speaking world, reaching major population centers with verse-by-verse exposition of Scripture. It also airs nearly a thousand times daily in Spanish, reaching twenty-three countries across Europe and Latin America. All of Dr. MacArthur's sermons are available at the ministry website (gty.org) at no charge.

Dr. MacArthur has written nearly four hundred books and study guides, including *The Gospel according to Jesus, The Gospel according to the Apostles, Ashamed of the Gospel, Twelve Ordinary Men, Truth Endures, Slave, Strange Fire, Parables, None Other, The Gospel according to Paul, Good News, The Gospel according to God*, and the MacArthur New Testament Commentary series. His titles have been translated into more than two dozen languages. *The MacArthur Study Bible*, the cornerstone resource of his ministry, is available in English, Spanish, Russian, German, French, Portuguese, Italian, Arabic, and Chinese.